T·H·E
NEW YEAR'S OWL

Encounters with animals, people & the land they share.

by Susan Hand Shetterly

Etchings by Robert Shetterly, Jr.

YANKEE BOOKS

A division of Yankee Publishing Incorporated, Dublin, New Hampshire

Designed by Eugenie Seidenberg

Yankee Publishing Incorporated
Dublin, New Hampshire
First Edition
Second Printing, 1987
Copyright 1986 by Yankee Publishing Incorporated

Essays in this book have appeared in the following publications: "Sea Stars," "Dragonflies and Nighthawks," and "October on the River" in *Yankee*; "Lorado's Marsh" and "Great Horned Owl" in *Habitat*; "Cait's Coons" in *Down East*; "The Bats of Summers Past" in *New England Monthly*. "Ida's Fields" was adapted from "Meadows Have a Million Lives" in *National Wildlife*, copyright 1984 by the National Wildlife Federation. All other essays appeared in *Maine Times*, except for "Git Along Little Dogies," "Dig It," "The Frog," "Syruping," "Woodcocks," and "Factory Days," which have not been published before.

"Tell Me a Story" copyright 1969 by Robert Penn Warren. Reprinted from AUDUBON: A VISION, by Robert Penn Warren, by permission of Random House, Inc.

Excerpt from "How to See Deer," copyright 1975 by Philip Booth. Reprinted from AVAILABLE LIGHT, by Philip Booth, by permission of Viking Penguin, Inc.

Library of Congress Catalogue Card Number: 86-50714
ISBN: 0-89909-115-6

To Cait and Aran
who have helped me to see
To Trav
who taught me to write

Foreword

Naturalists, like chess masters and fiddle virtuosi, tend to be a single-minded lot. At an early age many of them slip down the rabbit hole into their private wonderlands, and what they find there becomes almost their sole preoccupation for the rest of their lives. The matters of everyday human existence intrude as a nuisance at worst, at best an irrelevance.

I find it easy to sympathize with those who cop out on our concerns or, in George Crabbe's words, "grow unfitted for that world, and dote." Yet some force (inertia?) keeps tugging me back to that even greater illusion, "reality." I would like to lose myself in the mountains or on a rockbound island for a year, but then I would fall to wondering how the Dodgers were doing, or begin to miss a good Bordeaux with my dinner. After a long hike in the woods, the sight of a farmhouse or church steeple in the distance seems to me as satisfying and "natural" as the eyrie and remote waterfall I've left behind.

Susan Shetterly is my kind of naturalist. The human figure — and its concerns — are always a part of her landscape. I find wildness there, but also a deformed robin in the study and an ill-mannered gorilla at the zoo. And a small boy who dares the shivers to go with his parents on a chilly night in early spring and dip smelt from a village brook.

Our author watches gulls with a naturalist's keenness but then goes further, linking their winter habitat, the town dump, to the summer nesting island: "Although the dump is miles away, it rides like a phantom demon on the island's back." When she detects a great horned owl in the dark, she feels a surge of fear for her cat (though she is aware that the one kills as mercilessly as the other).

Nor does Susan Shetterly's heightened sympathy for animals blind her to the animosity and fear that is always there between us and the unhuman (or what Henry Beston called "those other nations, caught with ourselves in the net of life and time"). Her work in animal rehabilitation often reflects the unpleasant consequences of that wary relationship. But the antipathy can be very funny, as you will find when you read about her attempt to make friends with an ape, or about her mother's maternal instinct disintegrating in a swirl of batwings.

But Susan Shetterly can isolate her subject too, and then we witness a poet analyzing a strip of earth as if through a microscope. Her essay, "Coatue," is as gemlike as the Nantucket it describes — as finely honed a piece of nature writing as I have read in a long time. Hers is a Quaker island, Quaker-colored, yet jeweled and enameled with plants set in the sand in veins of dark, lacquered red, or "scattered like trinkets forgotten by a child." Among them grow brown saltwort, orache, and the pale sea rocket. "And everywhere, like Quaker elders, they toned things down."

Even here, she plays on the antiphony that brings human culture into concord with wildness. She and Robert go to Coatue Point before dawn to look out from the barrier beach into an ocean of darkness. "We waited for sunrise," she writes, "as if waiting for an immense animal to open an eye."

That is what the Shetterlys' book is all about. The world of wild things stares at them steadily, and two unique humans register the stare with an acuity rare in modern life. They look right back at it, seeing to the heart of wild lives and, mingling their impressions with intelligence and emotion, reproduce for us the essential aspects of those lives.

Here, then, is a book about eyes, about vision. But enough from this quarter; there is no need for anyone to stand in these artists' light. In a moment, you will be seeing for yourself.

– Frank Graham, Jr.
Field Editor
Audubon

Acknowledgements

This book could not have been written without Robert, my husband and its illustrator, who encouraged me through hard times and read so many drafts. The stories here belong to us both.

I want to thank Peter Cox, the editor of *Maine Times*, who first published many of these essays, and whose support I am grateful for, and Tim Clark for his sensitive, patient editorship and his energetic faith in the book's message. Special thanks to Bill Townsend for reading the manuscript for scientific accuracy, and to Sherman Merchant for his generous help whenever I had a question.

These etchings and essays owe a great deal to the people of Gouldsboro, especially Prospect Harbor, and the land and its coves they hold in trust.

Introduction

Tonight the snow had a perfect grain to it. As the sun slipped down, I skied through the woods, our terrier running behind me in the tracks. The trail across the stream drops steeply. I leaned into it, coasted down and up the other side, hitting the rise with a little, unavoidable hop.

The light behind the leafless branches of the oak and ash trees was a strip of narrowing pink becoming thinner and darker and more intense. Deep rose. Orange. Then a streak of blood red against the hills.

Abruptly, we heard coyotes. *Yip, yip, yip, yip* and five howls, one after another, suspended in the darkening air. The dog whined softly. I slid along the trail, faster now, concentrating on the turns between the black trunks of the trees. The voices rose again. From nowhere. From everywhere. For a brief time, they swallowed us.

We emerged to the lights of the house spilling onto the snow. The singing had stopped. I bent down and felt the dog tremble. Here, in the safety of her dooryard, she turned to face the woods and gave a brief, gratuitous growl.

The theme of these essays is connection. I believe it is the elemental stuff: connection between people and animals and the land they share. In the midst of casual and enormous destruction, it offers each of us a decent sense of who we are. The crazy voices of coyotes in the woods keep us sane.

The events of these essays range across a decade or more, and sometimes go back to my childhood. With the exception of a few, their focus is the Maine coast where I live. When Robert and I chose the sixty-acre woodlot outside Prospect Harbor in Gouldsboro, our son, Aran, was less than a year old. For ten years we learned to live there, cutting wood, burning kerosene lamps, gardening, and working odd jobs. Our daughter, Cait, was born. And it was there that I became a licensed wild bird rehabilitator. We moved once more, to another woodlot, outside another coastal town. It makes no difference which town these essays start from, really; their purpose celebrates the wildness left in this diminished land.

Tell Me a Story

(A)
Long ago, in Kentucky, I, a boy, stood
By a dirt road, in first dark, and heard
The great geese hoot northward.

I could not see them, there being no moon
And the stars sparse. I heard them.

I did not know what was happening in my heart.

It was the season before the elderberry blooms,
Therefore they were going north.

The sound was passing northward.

(B)
Tell me a story.

In this century, and moment, of mania,
Tell me a story.

Make it a story of great distances, and starlight.

The name of the story will be Time,
But you must not pronounce its name.

Tell me a story of deep delight.

Robert Penn Warren

WINTER

The New Year's Owl

On New Year's Eve, neighbors arrived on our doorstep carrying a wounded owl. We were on our way to a costume party. Tactfully, they ignored the shapeless fedora Rob wore as he let them in and the chartreuse necktie that hung in a rumpled knot from his collar. They did not comment on my red corduroy chaps with fringe, nor did they express surprise at the sombrero perched on my head like a wind-ruined haystack. The woman gently handed me the bird, wrapped in a towel.

Her grandson stood beside her. Walking diffidently behind them was her husband, who had brought the owl in off the snow. For long stretches of his life he had been a lobsterman, scallop-dragger, and fisherman. He was a two-pack-a-day man who eked out a living during lean times with odd jobs and spent the winter evenings in front of his TV. Although none of us knew it yet, he had lung cancer. Tonight he was keenly interested in the fate of the owl.

We spread newspapers on the kitchen table and turned the bird onto its back, covered its face with the towel, and held its feeble talons together with a leather glove. The grandparents and grandson leaned forward to look as the bird's wing flopped open. A spear of ragged bone sprang up from the humerus of the left wing.

"Compound," I said flatly, knowing that the chances of this owl ever flying again were almost nil and that we would be late for the party.

They left. The owl lay unprotesting as Robert and I took off our hats and began to work. The wound was old. We made it bleed again. The airy feathers of the bird's chest lifted and fell beneath our fingers. The owl had probably flown against an electric wire, and the force of its wingbeat had snapped the bone. Once, years ago, watching golden

3

plovers rise off an autumn field in Nantucket, we saw one hit a wire on the upstroke and somersault back to the ground. Beyond it, a wing drifted away like a lost kite.

After disinfecting the owl's bone stubs, we pivoted them until they fit together, braced them, and taped the wing to the body. We turned the bird over and sat it on a towel rack. Its feet adjusted to the size of the rack's dowel and clamped. Its gray eyelids closed down slowly and slowly drew up again. It was a barred owl, but it seemed to weigh no more than a robin. We cut strips of lean beef and dipped them in milk. Owls love milk, or so many rehabilitators believe. We pressed a strip against the side of its beak. It turned from us and snapped lightly, as if we had broken a rule of owl etiquette which, with frail dignity, it was prepared — this time — to overlook. We dipped and pressed again. A drop of milk slid between the mandibles. The owl tasted, swallowed. It closed its eyes, barely opened its beak, and took the meat. After that, the feeding was easy; the owl, ravenous. But it never rushed. Each piece was carefully considered.

The barred owl is an eastern, forest-loving bird. The large, liquid brown eyes, surrounded by luxurious plumage, make it look like a soft toy a child might take to bed to keep away bad dreams. It does have a reputation for being gentle. And this, to some extent, is justified. It is not an aggressive bird like the great horned owl, nor is it as skittish to handle as the short-eared. But in the wild, it feeds on smaller owls when it finds them, and during daylight hours has been seen hurtling through the air, locked in combat with a large hawk.

The barred is a hunter of the half-light. You may see it drop from a branch and begin its low, soundless inspection of the woods roads and the fields just before the sun goes down. The bird tends to set its time against the great horned owl, which is the absolute ruler of the dark. When there are no nesting great horneds in its territory, the barred owl yaps and chuckles. Sometimes it yowls like a house cat or laughs in a dry wheeze like an old man telling a joke to himself.

Birds that must cope with northern winters often go hungry during periods of heavy snow. When the voles and mice tunnel close to the ground and the varying hares turn nearly as white as the snow itself, when the fish rest in deep water beneath the ice and the snakes curl together in cold sleep, there is precious little for owls to eat. In spring, people have found them frozen in open sheds, mere husks, the skin tight over the bladed sternums.

But hunting season, not winter snow, may be the barred's greatest enemy. Because they are curious about people and alert during daylight hours, the barreds will sometimes follow hunters through the woods, bobbing their large heads and peering down from the tops of trees. Irresistible targets.

The New Year's owl was recovering nicely. It had escaped the large screened box in my study and now perched alternately on my typewriter and on the windowsill. Things were beginning to smell of owl and dead mice, so we made a compromise of sorts: the room was blanketed in newspapers and two perching logs were set astride my table. I moved out. In the evenings and early mornings, we could hear talons ticking across the floor and the scooting and rustling of newspaper sheets. I found disgorged pellets, tight wads of fur and bone, discreetly lodged in my poetry rewrites and old high school letters.

A body mends itself in much the same way disease destroys it: in secret, constant activity. At the wing break, a wash of calcium was laid down cell by cell. In six weeks we removed the splints. A hard knot of bone had formed. Soon, other cells would be brought to bear on the excess bone, eating away at it until once again the humerus lay straight beneath the muscle sheaths and the skin.

When released from the tape, the wing curved cleanly along the bird's side. I was astonished. It looked too good. Within a day the owl was flying, thumping against the windows, ready to leave. But first we had to find out whether the mended wing could sustain the hunt. An owl strikes with its talons. At the same instant, it backpedals, using its wings to draw away from the impact. The pressure on each wing is extreme.

We devised a method to see if the wing had sufficiently recovered. The owl ate mice supplied by the Jackson Laboratory in Bar Harbor. We kept packs of them in plastic bread bags frozen into a snowbank on the north side of the house. After defrosting one, we tied a length of black thread to the tip of its tail and laid it on the newspaper in the owl's room. The thread ran out under the door. We sat on the living room floor holding the thread as if fishing into an impossibly murky pond. We tugged. We heard it slip across the paper. We tugged again. Suddenly there was a crash from the other side of the door. The thread snapped. We rushed to the door and opened it. The owl grasped the mouse, looking up at us in shocked disbelief.

For a week we fished for owl before we were convinced that the

bird was ready for release. When the day came, we packed it into a cat carrier and drove to the field where it had been found. The grandfather and grandson joined us.

The field had once been an orchard. A few overgrown apple trees, gray and unraveled, lifted their bare branches before a line of spruce and fir. The sky was immaculate. We stood in a semicircle in a dust of snow. Rob held up the cage and opened the door. The owl shifted inside, then walked to the front of the cage. It peered out. It stepped onto the cage rim, flexed its shoulders, and flew. With slow, measured beats, it flapped over the thin snow and continued to the nearest tree, swung up to a center branch, and landed. We could see it, preening, as gray as the branches. It shook itself, as if shaking off every last human touch. Then the owl was gone.

As we walked back through the quiet orchard to the road, the grandfather looked as if he planned to savor what had happened here, to turn it over in his mind and see again the wings reach out and take the air.

Git Along Little Dogies

We stood in the empty room, its hinged windows thrown open, its door open, and listened to white-throated sparrows naming, before dark, the borders of their territories. It was our first evening in the cabin, a structure built like an afterthought, surrounded by a ring of trees and miles of trees behind those. This was our place now, Robert's and mine and our eleven-month-old son Aran's.

The smell of earth from the garden we had turned that afternoon wafted through the windows although the air was still. I had forgotten how sweet the bloom of new earth can smell. Night filled in the spaces around the trunks of the trees, and moved into the house and out across the ragged field.

We spread our sleeping bags on a mattress and coaxed Aran to close his eyes. The dark seemed alive. It seemed to come and go, without touching, around us.

I was born in New York City. I suppose many children, dropped into that maze of asphalt and metal, that surge of pedestrians, spend time pondering the meaning of such an error. Meanwhile, we grow up looking out windows through traceries of pavement dust, looking beyond the alleys and the next apartment house to the acres of waving corn and prairie flowers we know are out there. Somewhere.

In the foyer of our Bleeker Street building, it was always dusk. The dark green front door with a brass gargoyle opened to the ghostly runner of Oriental rug, the table with a pitcher of silk flowers, and a Victorian mirror behind. The foyer smelled of new oil paint and mold. And in the early evenings, there was a faint whiff of dinners.

We of country persuasion console ourselves with daydreams. I dreamed of deep, still forests that smelled like pine needles, of prairies where the sun beat on the long and rolling grasses, and of watering places where the sun dissolved to the bottom and I could see long-snouted fishes hiding in the reeds. I dreamed of riding for miles on my pinto named Paint, with a good hard rain beating down.

One spring, I asked my father to buy me a Hopalong Cassidy outfit for Easter instead of a new dress. To his credit, he did. He took me to Macy's and let me pick it out: hat, spurs, boots, string tie, shirt, pants, belt, badge, holster, and gun. I wore it to St. Luke's on Easter morning and noticed, with considerable pride, how the candle of the leading acolyte reflected in the silver rivets of the holster and the moulding of the gun's handle. For the next few months, I prowled the pavements not far from the front door, humming a cowboy tune.

On weekends, starting in March, my mother took me to Central Park. She liked to sit on the terrace of the restaurant in the gusty air and watch children with balloons and boxes of Cracker Jack, and their parents, fighting the wind. We ordered lunch. Afterward, she bought me a ticket to the carousel, where I searched out the same painted charger — white with a gold-and-green saddle — its mouth open and its teeth flared like a braying donkey's. I rode that horse solemnly, up and down and round and round, until the music slowed to a stop.

Before we left the park, we visited the cages. We saw the lion pacing back and forth behind the bars, as he had done ever since I could remember, with the same string of drool hanging from the mottled flesh of his mouth. We saw the one elephant standing in dead center of his square of wet cement, as if he couldn't believe he was there. Then the polar bears. They seemed bored to death flopped down on flat rocks across the moat of green water. The only animals expressing any joy were the seals.

Twice a year we made the journey to the Bronx Zoo. We saw great, black feathered birds with sleepy blue eyelids. We saw snakes tonguing the air of their glass cages. We saw fruit bats, and penguins on their simulated ice floes.

My father introduced me to the House of the Great Apes the year of my Hopalong Cassidy outfit. As he pushed open the door, we were enveloped in the smell, hot and intimate, before we saw them. A gorilla sat on a raised wooden platform, fiddling with its toes and shooting us looks of barely repressed contempt. Another gorilla shouldered its way back and forth in front of us, the shiny, wrinkled knuckles of its black hands pressing across the cement. It stopped, half-turned, then leaned away to stare at its fingernails, which were curled around the tips of the fingers like an old man's. It squatted to poke at an apple core. At the back of the cage lay piles of dung and spills of urine.

"Spit at him!" someone at the railing yelled. Four or five people spit. The ape, with a profound and other-worldly heaviness, ambled over. They spit again. It stamped its feet and groaned. It grabbed the bars with its hands and swung its head from one side to the other as if it had an unbearable headache. The people around me loved it. The gorilla's head went back. I stared, stunned by the gleaming canines and the pink pitch of the roof inside its mouth. Suddenly, it spit. Gorilla saliva dripped off the brim of my Hopalong Cassidy hat and slid down my cheeks. Everyone else — even my father — had jumped back. The gorilla spit again. Another direct hit.

My father reached out and yanked me away.

"Why did you just stand there?" he sputtered. "Why did you let him do that to you?"

I noticed, briefly, that my father's face had turned very red. As he wiped my face with his handkerchief, I smelled the gorilla spit; it smelled like rotten fruit. But I watched the cage. The gorilla scooted to the back, charged sideways, and crashed against the bars. It was yelling and spitting. I waited for the moment it would simply bend the bars, step out, and squeeze my father and me, one in each hand, until we oozed out of our skins, like bananas.

"Listen, Rob," I whispered. I shook his arm. The moon had risen, just a thin slice of it washing the floor in a gray-silver light. The sound moved. First, down on the driveway. Then, on the shed roof.

"It's a whip-poor-will," said Robert quietly. We crept to the door and eased it open. The bird flapped in front of us, then dropped like a moth onto the hump of granite in the middle of the garden, no more than ten feet away.

Whip-poor-will. A wispy, hoarse stammer — not enough to carry much.

Click. As if the bird snapped its tongue.

Whip-poor-will. Louder now.

Click. We held our breath.

Whip-poor-will. Whip-poor-will. Whip-poor-will. We sat in the sound as people sit in a downpour. If we had lifted our hands, the clear, strong syllables would have spilled through our fingers like rain.

Dig It

Rob and I chose Maine. It is a serious place. Why farm a woodlot here if you can get an acre or two of black Pennsylvania loam or an easy tract of river valley along the Ohio? I suspect that even back in the 1700s some people came to Maine for the same reason we did: land was cheap. All it took, we told ourselves, was brute, young strength and a willingness to shed the trappings of a life we no longer trusted.

It was 1970. The war and the civil rights movement had severed the last threads that held us to our childhoods. At the end of the sixties and the first years of the seventies, coming to the land was a journey made by many — a particularly American journey. We walked out the way Huck kicked off his shoes and set his tracks in the road past the school. No one could stop us. Pap prowled the Oval Office with his foul and lurching violence. The war went on and on and on. Let that raft slip away from the shore and drift 'round the bend! Let it lose the last view of town!

We arrived in a fishing village an early afternoon on one of the first days of June. Mist was rolling in from the Gulf of Maine, squeezing itself between islands and filling up the harbor. It swallowed one fishing boat after another until at last we couldn't see them. But we could still hear them slapping at their moorings. Drops of mist hung in the air. They were as cold as snow melt. On the dock a few men worked with quiet economy. They neither invited nor rebuffed us as we stepped over the lobster traps and around the coils of buoy rope. Up against the little harbor, houses perched on smooth granite swells. They were painted the same colors as the boats.

The first thing we did when we moved into the cabin on the woodlot near that harbor was to turn over half an acre of garden. By the end of the first week, an army of black flies had found us. Fly dope

13

couldn't dissuade them. Our faces were swollen and crusted with dried blood. Squashed flies hung from our hair.

By mid-afternoon, Rob and I were working in triumphant and separate sieges. The clouds of flies were as thick as harbor mist. We were feverish. We threw up at dinnertime. That night our blood bubbled through our bodies like lava down a mountainside. Grimly, the next morning, we grabbed our shovels and went out to the garden. No pesky fly stops a farmer.

We who were the first to "return to the land" — we pioneers — came most often in pairs, not groups, dropping into our second-growth woodlots and our alder fields steeped in the vigor of our choice. We didn't know much about the people whose generations lay in the kempt graveyards. We were often lonely.

Robert and I had heard about a man who had come to this county to homestead. One afternoon we drove over to his place, along a dirt road that ended in a wide rain puddle. Thin and knob-jointed, with a studied air of country and teeth missing from his upper jaw, he rounded his house and walked to us through a garden of car parts and boat motors.

"Yeah?" He sloshed into the puddle.

"We've moved into the cabin up on the Pond Road. We wanted to introduce ourselves."

"Yup." He leaned into the window on Rob's side. A vapor of fish wafted from his work pants. Behind the car parts, the house door swung open and a woman leaned against it, a lank-haired, tall woman in a faded cotton print with a face halfway between Appalachian hillbilly and Radcliffe undergraduate.

They were looking us over.

"Garden in?"

"We've just finished."

"Cut any wood?"

"No. No. We hadn't thought of wood yet."

"You'll probably burn green. How's the well?"

"Seems fine." I shifted our sleeping son onto my other shoulder. A fan of sunlight fell on his blond curls. He sighed. The man leaned comfortably against the open window, sucking on the spaces where his teeth had been. The woman approached the car.

"That well's polluted," she snapped. I gasped.

"But our son's been drinking the water!"

14

"You need a new well."

"A new well?" I stuttered. "How do we get a new well?"

"Dig it."

For a brief moment I thought she meant something like "Dig it, man. Groove on this country feeling." She meant the real thing.

"How?" I trembled.

"Shovel." She pivoted away from the car, strode into the house, and slammed the door.

That August we cut wood, and in September we banked a few fir boughs around the cabin to insulate it and settled in. We waited for winter as landscape. Something to walk on, something to skate on. Something to come into a warm house from. Cold, we thought, was a point of view.

By the beginning of February we had burned every stick. At night we put on hats and coats before bed. During an ice storm I reached for my boots and pulled them on under the covers.

We began to search the snow crust for dead wood the way starving dogs hunt bones. We snatched up every branch we could pry loose. And then we lopped off tree limbs, green and sappy, that bubbled in the cookstove as they burned. We cut birches at the snow line. Come spring, they stuck up like thumbs.

The first lesson the land demands we learn is vigilant attention. We were learning to respect it, as we would Goliath if we faced him, half-naked, with only three stones.

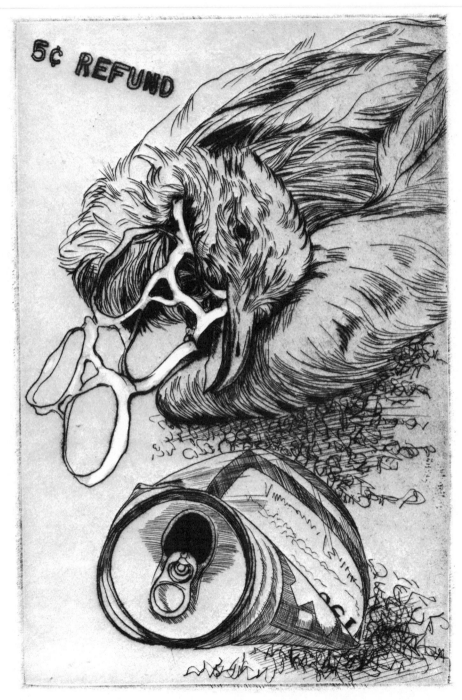

The Winter Dump

The dump is a foreign city. Along the road that leads to it, a crowd of papers and bread bags, caught in the dry field stalks, wave vigorously as if they had been waiting for us for hours, festive despite the sharp wind and the gritty rinds of old snow. The site itself is a low line of garbage hills where everything that is not too heavy flaps in wild welcome. If the wind is exceptionally hard, the coil of an old box spring jounces at the top of the frozen mound.

The far side of these rounded hills grades down in terraces to a small, sand-glutted stream. Things of permanence lie here, bracing and strengthening the whole. Bed frames ledge out, as do peeling doors, chair parts, a washing machine, and a table. Small openings perforate the hills like gypsy caves made cheerful with brightly colored bits and pieces.

The caves belong to rats. This swollen population of all-nighters drifts over the ravaged city after everyone else has left. In the sand, one can make out a tail track or a spatter of long-fingered prints from the aristocratic paws. A white cat sniffs at the caves, scratches open a greasy bag, noses through it, and yowls — an irritable, drawn-out sound.

The dump is less than an acre and a half. On its west side, a mix of sand and rock-studded fill lies in heaps to be bulldozed over the garbage. After the rain and the below-freezing nights, webbed prints of gulls stucco the fill.

Two species of gull commute to this dump: the herring gull and the greater black-backed gull. Audubon called the black-back "the tyrant king." It is larger and stronger than the herring gull and rivals the bald eagle's austere beauty. The jet mantle of the mature black-back elegantly sets off the pure white of the head, neck, belly, and tail. The bill is a dangerous blunt blade. The eyes, blond and pale, seem pitiless.

17

It takes four years for a black-back to reach mature plumage. The first three winters, its feathers are a warm, tortoiseshell brown; its bill is black. But every year both the breast and the bill lighten. At the final molt, the bird achieves its black back.

A first-year herring gull is the darkest gull at the dump, mahogany-headed and chocolate-flecked. Its bill is flesh-colored, tipped with black. Most herring gulls mature at three years; some take four. Those in their last juvenile plumage are disheveled-looking birds, the pearl gray backs sitting like loose saddles over the old brown feathers.

Gulls, like rats, have feeding hours: breakfast in the early morning and high tea at two. A steady entourage of trucks and cars backs up to the hills. The gulls give way to them, coasting briefly up and circling over. But they watch. Fat green lawn bags and the heavy three-ply garbage bags bounce onto the heap. Shreds of paper and unrecognizable, lumpy items get carried in the wind and slide over the ice to a stop. As soon as the vehicles speed away, the birds, like filings pulled by a magnet, converge. The concept "gull" disappears. What one sees is an agitated mass of wings, legs, and open bills. One hears an extravagant overlay of gull voices. It is the archetypal sound of plunder.

When the herring gulls jump on the bags, the air inside the plastic rolls like waves. The birds tease at the twists holding the bags closed. If a bag is a three-ply, a herring gull cannot rend it. When they find no way in, they claim it by squatter's rights. They sit down on it and wait. The garbage bags, like the skins of dead seals and porpoises and whales, are too tough for a herring gull's bill to pierce. But the bill of a black-back can penetrate. These tyrant gulls shoulder their way through the shrieking herring gulls, spread their feet, and jab. If a tear is made, all the birds seize on the wound and rip it wide.

The capacity of a gull's mouth is enormous. A doughnut or a stale roll is snatched up. In flight, the bird hitches the object back into its mouth, which stretches like the jaws of a snake ingesting an egg. Then the gull, with a shudder, swallows. A distortion swells the neck to one side as the lump of food makes its way down.

After feeding, gulls stroll the wan ice patches of the parking area and pace the fill. The youngest gulls mew to the adults, begging food. But it is winter and the instinct to care and feed is gone.

Always there is jockeying for position among the gulls. A threatening gull will stand tall, lift its neck, and lower its bill. The object of the threat usually shuffles aside or turns its head away and pokes vaguely at the ground. For no reason obvious to me, all the two hundred or more gulls will suddenly lift, screaming — a panic flight that takes them up and away for a few minutes. As they return, the cold air hisses with the sound of many wings. The birds land quietly.

As in any city, there are the walking wounded. One notices them first, dragging a wing or hobbling with a clenched foot drawn up. Last week there was an adult herring gull wearing a plastic six-pack holder like a bridled horse. The bird must have been rooting through a bag when the plastic strap slipped over its head and around its neck. But the bird was doubly stuck: another loop was embedded in its tongue, fixed tightly between its mandibles. Day by day, the gull weakened, not lifting anymore with the panic flight. It fought its way up the garbage and lay down, too tired to wrestle for the food it could not eat. Yesterday, I found its body, frozen in a patch of ice.

But this city of food and filth is generally kind to wintering gulls. Too kind. It does not cull the weak or the young the way life at the tide line would.

I watch the dump, but I am thinking of a summer island. Black ducks and eiders raise their chicks in the grassy hollows, petrels and puffins transport silvery fish down into the darkness of their burrows. The common and the Arctic terns brood their downy young. The gulls we save in winter destroy these birds. Although the dump is miles away, it rides like a phantom demon on the island's back.

And yet, the dump fascinates. The landscape around it is muted and stripped. Here beauty and ugliness, hunger and plenty, pain and pleasure spring up from the winter landscape in lively profusion. It is our Rio, our Marseilles.

Great Horned Owl

As steady as a metronome, the roof leak kept its time, even though the rain had stopped. Outside, the wind gusted in the branches of the red maples. We opened a window, and a breath of cold air entered the room, buffeting the flame in the kerosene lamp on the kitchen table. The sky had cleared and a gibbous moon glinted through the trees. On spring nights such as these, our house was a frail refuge, besieged by weather and dark miles of trees.

"Listen," I said to my husband, "there's a mourning dove cooing outside." Moaning rose from somewhere beyond the maples and the ring of spruces beside the field.

"The pitch is too low," Rob said after a pause. "Anyhow, doves don't coo in the dark."

"It's a dog," I decided. We opened the kitchen door to a deep howl. I pictured the animal, its neck outstretched, its mouth, as it cried, forming the letter "O." It sounded far away . . . chained, perhaps, and longing to be free at thaw-time.

It was, in fact, a great horned owl. Another bird soon hooted from the woods. And the first, from the neighboring field, returned the sonorous call.

We took down our volume of Edward Howe Forbush's *The Birds of Massachusetts*. "The great horned owl," we read by lantern light, "is the most morose, savage and saturnine of all New England birds. We can hardly wonder that certain Indian tribes regarded this fowl as the very personification of the Evil One. If he ever be moved to affection for any living creature, except, perhaps, for his mate, with whom he is accustomed to pair for life, the existence of such emotion is certainly not betrayed by any outward sign."

We read on, the dry pages of the book rustling like mice over fallen leaves. Outlaws were stalking the darkness beyond with a skill and cunning we did not possess.

"A farmer brought me a great horned owl one winter day that had killed his pet tom cat . . . . The cat was out walking in the moonlight . . . when the farmer heard a wail of mortal agony, and opening the door saw Mr. Cat in the grasp of the owl. Before he could get his gun and shoot the bird the cat was no more. Its vitals had been torn out."

"Our cats!" I whispered.

I plunged down the path to the garden, calling, the flashlight making a thin stab at the night. If it crossed my mind that my pets were predators like the owls, I wasn't inclined to dwell on it. I had become — provoked by the voice of a bird — one of those Americans who like their wilderness, but like it tame.

Working on my hands and knees along a row of cabbages one day that summer, I turned to see a great horned owl perched in a tree at my back. As I leapt up, it rose — wraithlike — and with one flap of its wings, disappeared. Sometimes at night when I walked through the high, wet grass to the garden, my cats would appear suddenly, their hair pearled with dew like a spider's orbed web at dawn. I would pick them up and carry them inside because I was afraid of the owls. But more often, the cats ignored my calls at night. I would find them when mist hung above the garden in the first light and the summer driveway was dry, trotting leisurely up to the house, satisfied with their time in the dark, it seemed, sure of themselves and their place here and their place out there.

There was an ice storm the following January. Alone in the house, Rob tended the fire in the cookstove and read by the lamp. The cats lay curled in their favorite chairs. At midnight, Rob rose to check the build-up of ice on the deck. He leaned out the door. Something yelped, brushed against his face, and beat away from the doghouse roof. He fell back as if punched. One of the owls had been waiting in the sleet and the wind, driven from the safety of the conifers by the prospect of cat.

Great horned owls claim territory and, unless driven from it by hunger, live all year within it, extending or reducing the boundaries depending on the abundance of prey. In February, the least likely month to start anything new in Maine, these owls begin their court-ship, filling the night with whoops and hollers. The male, the smaller of the two, shuffles after the female. Alighting on a branch close to her, he clicks his beak and bobs his round, wide-eyed face, pressing it close to hers. Then, stepping back and forth along the branch and fanning out his tail, he performs a choreography as stiff and mechanical as a break-dancer's. She does what so many female birds do: she ignores him. But this lack of enthusiasm only spurs his passion. He hurries off to return with a tidbit — a mouse perhaps, or a small bird. Daintily, she accepts the morsel from him and swallows it in one large gulp. She draws her eyelids down and raises them dreamily. Like an aphrodisiac, the food takes effect. She bobs and weaves along the branch as avidly as he, and they mate.

Great horned owls are not nestbuilders. They will settle into the ragged stub of a tall, dead tree or help themselves to squirrels' nests — and to the squirrels. They may usurp an old nest of the red-tailed hawk, the red-shouldered hawk, or the crow, and have even been known to preempt the rampart of the bald eagle. Since they breed early, before almost all other birds, they can take their pick.

One February, after a storm, I found a nest in a lightning-injured pine. The setting owl wore a cape of snow on its shoulders and head; snow wreathed the nest. Biologists believe that early nesting is necessary because incubating the eggs and raising the owlets takes so long. Not until October do the young wander from their parents' territory to begin independent lives. Also, winter affords the parent owls a choice of nests and a clean panorama — no deciduous trees or bushes curtain the activities of hares, squirrels, or wandering skunks.

The female great horned owl lays two or more eggs and begins brooding immediately after laying the first. Her nestlings are born consecutively.

If food is scarce, the youngest and weakest perish. Usually only one fledgling survives into the second spring.

The down of a newly hatched owlet is fluffy and white like cotton plucked from a cotton boll. In three weeks the eyes lose their milky blue and begin to show that bold, yellow cat color. At this time, the first real feathers appear. But unlike fledgling hawks, which exercise their wings at the nest's edge and then launch themselves into short, ungainly flights, young owls have not practiced when they tumble from the nest at about six weeks of age. Though they look lost, they aren't; the adults continue to feed their owlets, calling to them, coaxing them up onto logs and into the safety of bushes. It is here — on the ground — that the young learn to overcome the fear of other creatures. They rehearse catching insects and holding food in their talons and ripping off pieces with their beaks. They jump and coast short distances, and eventually, they fly.

Owls, like most birds of prey, regurgitate compact, cylindrical pellets of indigestible fur and bones called castings. Those of the great horned owl are two or three inches in length. A close examination of the bones and beaks packed within the castings reveals what prey is most abundant in their territory at that time of year.

Great horned owls are opportunistic feeders. Almost any animal is fair game. Weighing between two and a half and three pounds, great horned owls have been known to attack seven-pound Canada geese. Though rodents and hares are the staple fare, weasels and skunks are common prey, as are hawks and other species of owl.

The owl's strength is in its short, feathered legs and its oversized feet. From the four toes of each foot curl sharp, tapered talons just under two inches long. When an owl hits its prey, the legs buckle, the tendons tighten, and the feet close like fists. Double ice tongs, the feet cinch around the prey. The only way to loosen a great horned owl's grip when it is determined to hang on is to forcibly straighten its legs. I have held a recuperating great horned owl on my arm and felt the talons lock as the bird settled onto the glove — a grasp one does not quickly forget.

Once I cared for a great horned owl that had attempted to kill a porcupine. I am quite sure it never ate its victim, for there were quills in its feet and chest; its face sprouted quills. Even its tongue was peppered with black quill stubs. The veterinarian who anesthetized the bird and removed the quills stopped counting after eighty.

Most people who have worked with great horned owls describe them as sullen and ugly-tempered. This one only snapped and hissed half-heartedly when I lifted it into a cage. How long it had lived like a pincushion, unable to eat, able to stand only after breaking off the points of the quills that stuck out of its feet, too weak to hunt, and, at last, too weak to fly, I have no idea.

I bent my head close to the owl's and made what I hoped were friendly sounds. I reached my fingers through the feathers of its head, between the feather tufts we call "ears," and massaged the loose, papery skin. The owl's eyes closed. Then, leaving it three defrosted mice with antibiotics down their throats, I latched the cage.

It feasted on mice, it preened, it healed. In a week, I moved the owl to a large cage where it could stretch its wings. I had no flight cage for it, and for reasons I can no longer remember, I was uneasy about flying it on a tether — jessing it. Its strength increased. Clearly an aggressive bird, it spoiled for a fight. It hissed long, sibilant expletives that reeked of damp mouse fur. Old Mouse Breath, we called it.

On a glimmering late winter day, I hauled it back to the woods where it had been found. Holding its legs in my glove, I let the owl look around, let it flap. It seemed strong.

I released it. The bird took to the air, beautifully plumaged, the colors of tree bark, of sunlight against the bark, and of shadows thrown by a spray of twigs. But it slid downward, landing on a fallen tree. It raced and stumbled over the snow crust and bounced up on a stump, then puffed out its feathers and snapped. The owl was only fifteen feet from me but I could get no closer.

The muscles of its wings must have weakened from its time in the cage. It wouldn't fly. If I chased it, it would thrash over the maze of downed trees just fast enough to keep ahead of me.

I sat in the melting snow under its gaze. Outraged, bellicose, it clung to the stump anticipating my attack as if I could lunge at it across two piles of brush. I unwrapped the last wet package of mice and laid them in the snow in a semicircle before the bird as if to appease an irritable god. I wanted the bird to live.

A moth flew between us. The wrong time of year for a moth, and the sun going down. A thread of light caught on one of its wings, which the owl and I noticed, before it snapped and the moth flew off and the sun did go down.

In the dusk I heard the owl hop from the stump and move along the underbrush. But those sounds mixed with the wind in the trees and soon I could not tell where the owl was anymore. It seemed as if the woods were all owl or all the bare, snapping branches of the trees.

Syruping

We dream sap. We sense it, logy in the roots and being drawn, ever so slowly up an inch or two, then slipping back. We remember the sloshy ease of the snow beneath, and the sudden shock of it over the tops of our boots. We smell mud. These are the symptoms. We have caught the madness.

In the corner of our kitchen, stacks of gallon cans with wire handles have been standing for two weeks. Cone-shaped steel spiles lie in a bucket. A pile of tin lids, sharp as razors at the corners, overlap like roof shakes and spread on the floor next to the drill. We check the outside thermometer hourly. It is March and we have better things to do, essential things. But one by one, they fall away. We watch the thermometer column climb in the sun like sap in a tree.

At forty degrees, everything changes. Palisades of xylem around a tree's heartwood respond in an ecstasy of vacuums. These thousands of cells sing the sap out of the roots and get us running into our boots and outside.

We have red maples on our land: more than a hundred of them ring the field and follow the woods road up into the five-acre grove. Their red buds, like a little child's cold fingers, shine in the spring sunlight. They are bog maples, adapted in good spirit to the sour peat and the granite ledges. Their sap is less sweet than that of the sugar maples, but some people who have tapped both say theirs has a finer flavor. Without question, it takes forty-five gallons or more of red maple sap to make a gallon of syrup.

We tap as many trees as we have buckets, starting around the south field and working up the old woods road. An early woodcock hiding under an alder whistles off across the snow. Overhead, lines of geese move north. At first, as we hear them approaching from the south, they sound like a growling in the sky. Then, above us, we hear their clear, brave calling.

Scar plugs from spile holes of other years hold smooth and tight in the trees' bark. Picking a spot to the side of the old holes, we scrape off lichens and lean against the drill. The bit rasps its way through the delicate sheet of cambium and the spongy phloem. For a moment, it spins. Then it catches, hitting the flow. A stain fans down the bark as we pull out the drill. Wood chips and sap clog the hole. Our daughter, Cait, cleans it with her finger and puts her finger into her mouth for a taste of sweetness. But it is like water. Almost like water. There is a tang to it, a promise of things to come.

Aran drives in the spile. Hammering the head of it so as not to dent the spout, he sets it at the back of the drilled hole. We rest the handle of the can in the spile's hook, adjust the lid so that it fits like a rain hat, and stand back to listen to the first drops strike the bottom of the can. In an hour's time, sap is playing in the grove like a steel band.

Now, as soon as the sun hits them, the trees begin to pour. Some, for reasons of illness or age, or more secret reasons (a certain tightfisted-ness, perhaps), dribble reluctantly into their cans. The better ones flow exuberantly. Three times a day, on a good day, we pull on our boots and haul the five-gallon pail out to the cans. We drag it back and forth from the full cans to the thirty-gallon storage drum.

Our feet are always wet. The snow is deep, but running with water underneath. Spare boots, their tongues hanging out, steam under the wood stove in the kitchen like a pack of sled dogs. We are caught in sap madness, and so are the noctuid moths. They crawl out of the chinks of maple bark where they have wintered, awakened by the charge of sweetness in the air. For a long time, they cling to the bark, letting the heat penetrate into the long winter's stiffness. They practice curling and uncurling their proboscises. They tremble their yellow-brown wings. Suddenly ravenous, they leap and plunge into the cans. Spiders that have overwintered in the bark stumble hungrily after the moths.

The first year we tried to make syrup, we boiled the sap in a pot on the cookstove. A fine lacquer candied our windows. The next year we boiled off in the field using a tub and a hasty arrangement of cinder blocks. Heat spread ecumenically across the field. The smoke was more circumspect. It coiled from the punky logs and curled down into the boiling sap. When we finished, we had four gallons of sweet soot.

This year we have fashioned a three-sided syrup shed, open to the south, and equipped it with a box stove of fairly ample top and two gleaming steel trays that used to house experimental mice at Jackson Laboratory in Bar Harbor. A year's worth of scrap wood leans against the east wall of the shed. It is an assortment of board ends and dry rot. For months it has been soaking up every rain and every thaw. It sits in a sour, parsimonious lump. We pry it apart. We coax a few lumps into the stove. If we are lucky, it burns. If we are not, a delicate balance between tomorrow's warmth and today's syrup begins. To give heart to the fire, we might borrow from our split hardwood at the house. It waits on the porch, dry to the core, a precious stack turned and ready for the cookstove inside. Perhaps just one. Another, to give it strength. The fire beats red. The pans abandon themselves to a rolling boil. White billows break against the ceiling and the dark smoke rises up the stovepipe and away through the branches of the trees.

We used to have a candy thermometer, but gave it up. We prefer to study the color and the taste. We dip a spoon into the pan; it comes away with a small measure. All four of us critique the depth of color. With pursed lips, so as not to suck the spoon empty, we each take a taste, letting it rest on the tongue.

The sap boils darker and sweeter in the pans. The air turns cold. The flow in the trees slows and stops, and soon there is no sound from the cans. But the boiling goes on into the dark. Sunset is a weak pulse dying behind the trees. The dark comes rising after it like water up the trunks. Soon the only light left beats from the heart of our fire. It shines out across the quiet night.

All is still except for the crackling fire and melt water running under the snow. By flashlight, we fold cheesecloth across the mouths of quart jars. Robert tips the pan and the heavy liquid ribbons through the cheesecloth into the first jar. Then another. And another.

There is nothing left to do but scrape out the pans and twist the layers of cheesecloth into sugar tits. Two for each child. Sleepily, they sit on a log together and suck the syrup from the cloths. Tiny pieces of bark and twigs and lichens are caught in the weave, and probably parts of a hungry spider, and all of a moth's wing.

Ida's Fields

The day our fire department burned Ida's house, smoke carried from the rotted timbers and cracked linoleum and old cedar shakes. Ida was dead, and the house with its caved-in kitchen floor and ruined roof on that long stretch of empty road was considered a hazard by the town selectmen. We could smell the fire from our place and see smoke through the trees. By nightfall, bulldozers had pushed the charred rubble into the cellar hole and covered everything Ida had owned with a clean layer of dirt. Everything, that is, but her fields.

While she was alive, Ida did not let anyone walk those fields. It was rumored that if she caught you on them — and she was vigilant — she'd be looking at you down the barrel of a 12-gauge. She wore a nylon wig that looked like a brush fire flaming out of control, and beneath it, her face was a sour pucker. She died at ninety-three. That last year, she lived in one room of the house and spent her days perched like a caged bird at the window that looked out on the lovely roll of the fields.

I have walked them at least a hundred times since her death. It is one field, actually, folded into five parts. At the fold lines, streams sing out in a January thaw. In the spring, they flood. But by August, they have vanished. As the field drops south toward the road, a line of granite breaks through it, as sharp as the vertebrae on the spine of a large, old animal. Ten apple trees grow on either side.

The trees are more dead than alive. But every spring, a few branches leaf out and ruffle in the wind. Their small bouquets drive the bees to fits. The trunks and main branches are riddled with sapsucker holes, an arrangement that is precise and measured. The birds perforate the cambium layer of the trees. Beetles and moths and their eggs and larvae find refuge in this decay. On winter days, hairy woodpeckers chisel off plates of bark as they hunt the insects.

31

Summer nights the cries of loons issue from the lake across the road like rising water carrying in its eddies all the unspeakable sadness of the earth. A whip-poor-will calls from the granite ridge.

A fox trail leads to the dense wickets of last year's grasses where white-footed mice and voles have their runs. Then the trail veers to follow the boundary of the field. It disappears into the woods. Ida permitted no trapping, so for generations the foxes, which denned where the woods break into a scree of granite at the old town line, kept to their traditions. Foxes walk and trot with their feet lifting and touching down one behind another. That is why the trail looks at first like a natural parting of the grasses.

A section of old cedar fence disintegrates along one side of Ida's field. The rails and posts brace into the dirt, hollowed with rot and wrapped in a soft footing of cushion moss. Beyond this lies a common testament to a man's work: a pile of fieldstones. Encrusted with a fungus called rock tripe, the stones look as if they could be rubbed between the fingers of one hand and crumbled into dust.

Ida's husband cleared this land when he was young to pasture cattle and horses. He cut trees and pulled stones and planted the wild field in clover. But today the field gives way to old habits. The alders have crept back. Poplars have flung lines of saplings across the grasses.

The lower jawbone of a horse protrudes from the ground by the fence. The bone itself is fragile, but the front teeth are firm in their sockets and the yellow enamel on the molars is polished and hard. Would Ida have remembered this horse? Remembered whether it lay down and died here? Perhaps it was buried where I am standing. In a sudden frost heave or a guttering spring thaw, the earth delivered to the surface this one relic. Mice have come to gnaw at the bone. Their teeth marks flute its edges.

On the northwest corner of the field, thatches of brown orchard grass grow tall. Sometimes the grass is pressed down in large elliptical shapes where deer have rested. They keep their ears to the sounds coming up from the south. They lift their heads, which are the color of the grasses, and peer down. At a hint of danger, they arise and slip back between the trees. If you see them at all, they seem to be sporadic gusts of wind, blowing the grasses.

I suspect that Ida saw them. Too old to move, to eat, her voice too old to say a word straight, but keen-eyed as a hawk those last days sitting at her window, I bet she counted every one.

SPRING

Woodcocks

They exploded up from the weeds. One hit the side of the out-house and slid down it to the ground like a cowboy knocked cold in a frontier bar. Two or three slammed through the branches of the firs. Baby woodcocks. They had been out with their mother for their first evening of probing for earthworms in the lower garden, not one of them seasoned to danger.

Their mother had walked away from it, most likely. We hadn't heard her flight. Looking like a patch of fallen leaves, she had vanished into the dusk. She was probably crouched nearby, listening.

We shone the flashlight along the outhouse wall. There the little woodcock lay, its wings spread, suspended in a net of wild raspberry canes. I picked it up. The bird was not stunned. Nothing was broken. Under the flashlight, its eyes gleamed, dark and expressionless. Its long bill was translucent, as if the adult coloring had not poured into it yet. Its legs were pale; I could feel the pliant bones of the feet against my skin. Beige baby fluff poked through its dark brown feathers on the top of its head.

It turned around twice in the cup of my hands, sat down, and snuggled in.

"So much for life on the wild side," Robert laughed.

The night had fallen truly. A great horned owl began its muscular call from the pasture across the way.

"This is your place," I told the silent, entrenched bird. "You belong here."

"Let's put it down in the bog," Robert suggested. The bog was on the opposite side of the patch of firs. The other young birds had flown in that direction. We walked over, and I set the bird on the damp sphagnum footpath. It wobbled slightly, as woodcocks do, as if a small

35

pendulum swung somewhere inside it. It peered down that narrow path arched over with branches of labrador tea and sweet fern. Step by step, it advanced into the darkness, the banner of fluff sticking up from the top of its head. The darkness took it back without a sound.

That first spring in Gouldsboro, Robert and I would stop by the upper garden in the wash of a melting sunset and listen to a woodcock perform its mating ritual in the near field. For decades, birders had debated how a male woodcock makes the noises he does.

The *peent* there was never any question about. That sound erupts from the woodcock's throat. As he rocks back and forth on his mating turf, you can see the *peent* well up and bounce out like a large burp. It almost knocks him over.

What happens next is the hard part. He leaps into the air and begins to spiral. In wider and wider circles, higher and higher into the dusk, he disappears, making, all the while, those wheezy, dry twitters. You would think he was headed for the moon the way some moths, dazed by the lunar light, fly off and drift, lost in the upper atmosphere. But the woodcock stops. He hovers at the summit of the gyre and from him rushes a loud and waterlike three-note song. Zigzagging, he falls. He rides the air down. You see him for an instant, a black dot, a plunging piece of burnt-out star, before he falls into the shadows, landing where he began.

"He was singing as he went up."

"No. That's wind through his wings. He's singing as he comes down."

With the aid of flash cameras and sound impressions, ornithologists have resolved that wings create the spiral song. The bird sings as it falls. That should settle it, I suppose. Simple enough.

But out in the dark at the edge of a field, facts can turn slippery, can fall away like fishes through our fingers. Was it only the making of the sounds that we wanted to understand? Those pulsing, sweet, crazy sounds? Or was there something else?

Woodcocks are early migrants. They come, like the vanguard of robins, a week or so ahead of the decisive thaw, when the weather can still turn. Eager for everything that spring means to them, these birds fly at night into the cold, immaculate air, over the snow patches and the pointed firs. They gamble. They stack all their chips against one turn of the wheel.

One year, the first week in April, the snow that had fallen more than a foot during the night lacquered over in a sudden rise, then drop, of temperature. Locked beneath it, the earth and the wild seed were inaccessible to migrating fox sparrows. They flocked to the feeders, trying to scratch out millet swept off the platforms by the wind and buried in the ice. Kicking away at the crust, I spread new seed in soft, powdery hollows. As I turned back to the house, I noticed a woodcock walking in front of the fir boughs banking the side of the kitchen. The house's warmth had spread beyond the pile of firs and a tiny snowless line marked it off. An inch or so of bare, hard earth. It looked like a piece of brown ribbon. Along it stepped this woodcock, setting its feet meticulously within the line, as though to step out of it, even to place its foot on the border, would invite destruction. As I approached, it whistled away into the ice-slick tangle of alders by the stream.

All that week the ice remained. It settled in, grew harder. The coldest wind blew across the jinxed landscape.

They died like Big Foot's people at Wounded Knee, spread across the white, cruel fields, their legs and their wings and their heads at irregular angles as if they had jolted with the sudden discharge of life. I gathered up woodcocks and dug graves in the snow, scratching at the leaves and sticks underneath. I could not fold them or set their heads on their breasts so that they looked as if they had fallen asleep: they had not fallen asleep. They had suffered. Their bodies insisted upon it. So I scooped large holes in the snow, scraped at the earth, and lay down the evidence of a cold spring.

At night, I woke. In the dark, those woodcocks stuck up inside me like broken bones. Layers of my wakeful attention washed over them. They are with me still, their shapes unforgettable, as if fixed in shale. Split apart the brittle sheets and there they are, like a nest of Archaeopteryx. But they are only woodcocks, fossilized.

Smelting

At Whitten Parrit Stream in Steuben, men and women stand on the banks. The trees around them block the moon's full light. You can see the ends of their cigarettes, how the little points of fire glow brightly when they puff. You can hear their nets swish back and forth in the water. It is as if they had gathered here to row, with long-stemmed oars, a heavy black-timbered boat out into the bay.

They are dipping for smelt, the small fish that ride into the streams on a full tide these May nights. The fish race from pool to pool up to their spawning beds. Occasionally, a net lifts out of rhythm. A smelt slaps down into a bucket.

In our town next to Steuben, there is a brook called Popeye. In late May, it carries the last of the snow melt out of the woods. You can jump over Popeye, holding a smelt bucket in one hand. This time of year, its water pitches and tosses above the banks. It splashes through the culvert under the tar road and then runs, quicksilver, down a slope to the bay.

The bay rises to meet it. On the broad surface of the salt water the moon's path lies straight and glinting. It sweeps into the mouth of Popeye.

Aran, who is four, dreams of smelt fishing as soon as the first thaw loosens the ground. He likes to be awakened after dark. He likes to dress against the cold. Our dip net has been reinforced with a coat hanger and some cheesecloth, but it works, or at least we have never seen the smelt swim in one side and out the other.

We stand at the stream like the trees that stand here, in silhouette: three trees of staggered height, dressed to the teeth and shivering. Our flashlight glows feebly. The air is as cold as the side of a bell.

Generations of people from our town have pulled generations of these sweet-tasting smelt out of this water. Before them, the Passama-quoddies did; they knew what nights the fish might risk a journey against the current. Somewhere along its banks, somewhere higher up and into the woods, a mink may step from stone to stone, waiting. A raccoon might feel alongside a large rock, midstream, where the fish like to hide. Leaning from its perch on a fallen log, a barred owl might peer into the water as if it were trying to read the gravel bed.

The scientific name for the smelt is *Osmerus mordax*. *Osmerus* refers to its smell, which is sweet and green, like sliced cucumber. *Mordax* means bite. The smelt has a lower jaw that protrudes beyond the upper. From each jaw sprouts a set of honed teeth.

Smelt are creatures of the bays and waters off the inshore islands. They are anadromous, which means that they move from salt water into fresh to spawn. But they are adaptable. Some are found in warm, reedy ponds. Landlocked populations thrive in some fresh lakes with deep, cold bottom strata.

At six inches in length, with large, loose scales and a pronounced cleft in its tail fin, the smelt appears fragile. Unlike the salmon, it cannot breach and heave itself over obstacles. As it climbs, it seeks temporary refuge on the lee side of rocks and submerged logs.

Mature males begin the run, fighting upstream until they swim above a wide span of clean gravel. As midnight approaches, the females nose at the mouth of the stream. One by one, they ascend. A rash of blunt points has grown on the scales of the male fish. A female enters the spawning bed and he presses against her. The points hold her to him. The fish do not slide away from each other in the fast water. In unison, their tails beating a slow pulse, they spawn. The eggs sink to the gravel in a cloud of milt.

Before dawn, the smelt stop fighting the current. They let themselves be drawn back into the bay, where they regroup and swim away.

We skim our light over the streambed and, like the raccoon, force our hands into the numbing water, feeling along the rocks' shapes for a pulsing fin or a sprinting sleek body. But it is still too early. The fish must be waiting beneath that long run of moonlight. We extinguish the light. Taking turns, we dip the net into the current and bring it out and back and dip again. The sound of the mesh through the water and the water shedding from it as it moves above the stream are rhythmic, lulling. The moon catches in the drops as they fall. It is a long, bone-cold time.

Suddenly, the rhythm breaks. The net rasps against a rock. Aran lifts it high and thrashing. When first caught, a smelt is the color of melting ice: blues and polished silver. The tones fade as it dies.

Too soon, our bucket is full. The water has stiffened our fingers; we can barely hold the net. At our feet in the churning current, the ancient, imperative ritual continues. Smelt thrust steadily past us like small black whips.

Come morning, we will eat smelt fried in cornmeal. Then this ritual of ours, which leans completely on theirs, will be over.

Robins

The pop of the cork fractured the air, and champagne foamed into our glasses. We carried them to the cage in the bird room, where a blue eggshell lay in two ragged pieces. We listened. Something brushed against the silence. It was the voice of a newly hatched bird.

"To Big Bob and Bert," Robert intoned, "and their young." We drank. The two robins inside the cage watched us quietly. Big Bob sat tight to the leaning tower of her nest and Bert kept vigil by her side. We had bought the bottle of champagne eleven days before, after we noticed the first egg. Checking off the days against the calendar, we watched Big Bob feed, return to the lip of the nest, sway from side to side, and settle in until only her head and tail showed above the cup.

Captive breeding has become high art among wild-bird rehabilitators. One reads of peregrine young raised at Cornell, rare whooping cranes at Baraboo, the endangered brown pelican at St. Petersburg. But the event we toasted was not newsworthy. Outside, the lawn was alive with robins. There seemed to be more this year than ever before. Big Bob gently nudged her newborn and turned the three eggs still warm in the nest as we refilled our glasses.

The American robin is actually a thrush. It was named by settlers who were homesick for the little Robin Red-breast of the English hedgerows. Most thrushes are spotted on the breast; robins lose the spots as they mature.

Before there were settlements on the prairies, when robins left their southern wintering grounds in early March they migrated up the eastern and western flyways. They flew over the central plains into the forests of Michigan and Wisconsin without stopping. Homesteading changed all that. Settlers planted fruit and shade trees to soften the vast, empty feeling the grasslands gave them. Robins began to stop at the trees and nest. Today they are familiar in every state in the contiguous United States and in Alaska.

There are two types of American robin, separated by genetic predisposition. The robin of the forests is a secretive, wary bird like its close relatives, the hermit thrush and the veery. The farm robin seeks out lawns and fields. By tilling and mowing, we make the insects and worms it requires easily available. This is the robin that is usually found and brought to me.

The story of the birds in the cage began in mid-July two summers ago when neighbors discovered a fallen nest. Inside, a young robin clung to its shattered cradle. When I picked it up, the nestling emitted a sweet *churp*. Its oversized beak opened and a blueberry glistened ripely from the back of its throat. There was blood on its wing, a tear from which a bone protruded against the line of feathers still wrapped in their sheaths. As I carried the bird and its nest to the car, the parents called from a tall white pine.

At home, Robert and I taped the wing. The bird took handling easily, occasionally opening its mouth, into which we dropped a berry. Afterward, it sat in the nest for three days, preening vigorously, dislodging sheath paring like pieces of old fingernail, and stroking the unfurling plumage that draped cleanly over its back.

Most robins are stalwart even when severely wounded. A warden once told me that a moose, when shot, assumes it is dead, even if only nicked. But a deer will run dead. Robins remind me of deer. The bird in the nest was cheery and — I almost don't dare say it — affectionate. It loved to be stroked. It loved to eat. It greeted anyone who entered the room with wildly appreciative cries. But it stayed where it was. At last, I lifted the robin and looked. Its feet were crippled. When I touched them, they showed no response. How could we have missed those feet when we set the wing?

I believe in the good death. I would not keep alive a creature who could barely move. Reluctantly, the next day I brought home a small, clear vial of chloroform. The bird's bright humor made me miserable. I waited for a day or two, as if I had options. Only chloroform made sense. And then one night Robert and I cut a thick piece of mat board into tiny leg braces, turned the startled bird on its back, and bound the toes open and the legs, to the first joint, straight. Although it was not yet healed, we removed the tape from the wing. The bird struggled and righted itself, its feet centered stiffly beneath it. Using the wings as

44

oars, it rowed itself across the floor. And still it was cheerful.

My little study was a hospital ward that summer, an odd, intense place with a waxwing, a kingfisher, and two kestrels living in their respective cages. The robin scraped over the floorboards and back again. It nibbled at my daughter's toes, which were small and pink and, I suppose, triggered the instinctive response that worms do. It whined — a thin, high, warbly whine — and one of us would pick it up and pat it until it fell asleep in our hands. Mysteriously, the legs started to mend.

When we removed the braces, the legs splayed but were strong. In the garden, we constructed an enclosure out of old window screens and rabbit wire and moved the robin to it. We released it to follow us across the rows of parsley and through the squash vines. It found out what real worms were. But by September, we couldn't let it into the garden anymore. Half-wild, it would not be touched. It watched the other robins feed and fly on. The squash vines died. In the mornings, frost lay heavy on the cover of the cage. The young bird's back lost its highlights and turned a gray-olive brown. The speckles of the breast wore away and the color became a pale orange-pink, like old bricks. She was a perfect specimen of a first-year female, even if she couldn't fly. We named her Big Bob.

At summer's end, robins assemble in huge flocks as they move south. Like blackbirds, and the passenger pigeons before, they gather on their wintering grounds in a chosen copse of trees deep in the woods. They follow each other there, in long, tapering flocks, squabble for a perch, and sleep like soft round fruits, upright on the branches. Few people have ever seen these enormous robin roosts. But those that have don't forget.

I brought home another robin that had been living in the general cage at the Cordelia Stanwood Wildlife Sanctuary in Ellsworth, along with the unreleasables left over from summer. The bird's body, like a face in a Dorothea Lange photo, seemed to survive by the force of spirit alone: the toes of one foot were stubs, the right wing almost entirely gone. Only a pink nub of flesh stuck out where it had been. The tail was jaunty, but it bore only one feather, as if on a rakish cap.

I lifted the bird into Big Bob's cage, and when it saw her, its thin shoulders drew together. Its sharp sternum beat with nervous breathing. After she had made certain that another robin was, in fact, sharing her space, she dashed to the food dish and ate everything in it. She picked up the last scattered currants. Her neck bulged with too much food. Heavily, she climbed to the new bird, grabbed it by its pink thumb, and heaved it to the floor.

For two days the new bird lived at her mercy. Then he began to stand up to her. Mouths open and hissing, they sparred with each other, tripping over the branches and, sometimes, falling together and thrashing on the cage floor. When the tiff was over, they preened. Or she might jump into her water dish and bathe as he sat on a branch above her and made splashing motions. Afternoons, they perched, and pecked invisible pieces of dirt from between their toes. If he picked at the right foot, so did she. If he changed to the left, she found something objectionable on her left foot. He yawned and she opened her bill, almost against her will, and yawned.

Through the plate-glass windows that winter, our robins looked out on the feeder at the flocks of grosbeaks and the marauding jays. The water never froze in their bowl. As the winter birds fought the terrible cold, the robins watched them idly, and bathed.

By March, the last storms hit with the quick perversity of retreating regiments. Inside the cage, the male, Little Bob, turned bold. He demanded first privileges at the food bowl and the entire span of his favorite branch. His breast bloomed a deep, brave red. The feathers of his head turned a sterner black. Big Bob fluttered near him.

One early morning Rob and I were sipping coffee in the kitchen, absorbing the sulky gray of another sunless, rainless day, when a death rattle issued from the bird room. It began as a slow, hoarse gasp — an intake of breath that sounded painful — and fell away in four clicks. Over and over came the gasp and the four carefully timed clicks. Little Bob was singing.

Young male robins in the wild hear the male parent sing. They have been known to practice what they have heard in wavery whispers. But they rehearse in earnest on the migration north the next spring. The first flocks of robins to arrive are bands of males singing and claiming territory. A robin marks his boundary with song the way a coyote or a wolf marks his own with urine. The robin sings a challenge to the neighbors.

Perhaps Little Bob was attempting what he remembered of a bird's voice at the Sanctuary, where he was raised. Or, perhaps, it was his rendition of jay call. To correct it, we dug out our Peterson tape and recorded "Page 125, American Robin: *Cheery-up, cheery-o, cheery-up, cheery-o, chup, chup, chup*" forty times on a blank tape. We played it back to him. The minute the recorder snapped on, he hopped to the end of the cage and waited. "Page 125." He cocked his head. As the song began, his throat pulsed and sweet, robinlike ripples issued from it. As soon as the tape stopped, he began his horrible, long intake of breath.

Despite her mate's discouraging appearance and distressing voice, Big Bob spent her mornings gathering pieces of straw, mounting to the highest branch, and dropping them. We cut down a Quaker Oats box and fitted it into the cage, stirred up some mud, and carried in what we thought a robin might like to use to make a nest. Both birds worked single-mindedly. Their nest, when finished, spilled out over the box. Big Bob laid two eggs and cautiously rested upon them. Little Bob stood at her side and sang.

It was a long wait. In A.C. Bent's account of the American robin, the female never incubates for more than fourteen days. Big Bob knew that, too. On the morning of the fourteenth day, she stood up, jabbed into the nest, poked a hole in each infertile egg, and threw them to the cage floor. Then she hopped to the water bowl and washed her hands of the whole thing.

Deciding that the birds might be stimulated by wind and rain and the sights and sounds — up close — of other birds and hoping that they might try to mate again, we carried the cage outside and braced it against the garage. Immediately, we found that their sense of territory extended to the whole bird room, not just to the cage. They were frightened. Little Bob flipped off his branch and landed with a thud to the cage floor. He flipped most of the day. By evening he had calmed a bit, and we looked forward to the next dawn.

But at daylight I found Little Bob's body lodged into a corner like the crushed hull of a dory. His head was gone and a leg ripped off. His bare flesh was flensed to the bone. A rat had pushed between the door and the jamb, and in his panic, Little Bob had almost certainly catapulted off his perch. Like a fallen standard, his only tail feather drifted in the water bowl.

We moved Big Bob to a tight cage. Perhaps it was time for her to molt, perhaps not, but her feathers fell out by the handful. And she slept.

I went back to the sanctuary, to the same cage where I had found Little Bob. A first-year robin with a permanent wing injury puttered over the litter. It was a light-colored bird, still speckled on the breast. It

seemed too brown for a male. But the crown of the head was dark, more emphatically marked than Big Bob's. On a hunch, I took it home.

Robins are flocking birds. It is stressful for one to be isolated. And yet, unlike geese that pair for life, a robin's loyalty is not to an individual, but to a territory.

I placed the carrier with the new bird close to Big Bob's cage. She awoke and shook. She peered into the carrier. The new bird approached the grid and looked up at her. They made low, introductory sounds. The next morning, we put the new bird into Big Bob's cage. She jumped down, ate all the food, grabbed the bird by its injured wing, and flung it to the floor. Everything was going to be fine.

We named the new bird Bert and started playing it the old tape the first of February. We imagined it turning him into a male if he wasn't. In our mind's eye we saw the *cheery-up, cheery-o* sliding into his ears, along the bright wires of his nerves, hormones pulsing, sending the beat through his body. For a month he stood very still and listened. Our hopes gradually faded. But the first week of March, he whispered. By the end of the month he sang the tape precisely in such a pure, loud whistle it brought tears to our eyes. As other males wrestled for our acre of yard, he let loose that crazy whinny that means, "Out of my way, you cringing cowards!" He sang and sang, and soon after, we bought the champagne.

It is September. The four young have been released. Bert proved an admirable father, feeding them in the nest and teaching them to hunt for themselves in the cage litter when they fledged. A week ago Big Bob refurbished the nest and laid two more eggs. She sits on them as if she were listening. He sings, but less forcefully now that summer wanes.

We are proud of these birds, our peregrines. From that dilapidated enclosure of their cage, they sent forth four wild birds, undiminished by the handicaps of their parents. The genetic legacy of Big Bob and Bert goes free.

White Pine

Slowly, inexorably, the earth is falling to quiet armies of flowering plants and broadleaves. The conifers, rulers of ancient forests, are declining over the continents. But you wouldn't know it here. At least a hundred white pines spire above the birches on this small acreage we own. And an old tree, a true cathedral pine, once graced the edge of a clearing. Its presence moved us to buy this land and build.

Twenty years ago, cutters thinned our woodlot; the pines were spared. Now they impart to us a half-sense of what this coast might have looked like when the first timber cruisers, working for the king, dragged their rowboats up onto the salt grass in Morgan's Bay.

After a white pine begins to bear seed, it produces a cone crop every five years. Stubby yellow fingers cluster at the branch tips. They hold pollen. Higher up, female flowers receive the pollen and eventually ripen into cones. In a bearing year, the air around white pines is heavy with the yellow dust.

In early New England, forests of white pine spread out behind the shore-bound colonies as far as the eye could see, as primeval as one's mind could imagine. The dominant forest tree in most places, these giants held the woods in a still and silent trance where sunlight filtered down and the needles on the floor gave off a hot and pungent smell. Fastened to the thin glacial till, they could live nearly three hundred years and easily overcome trial by lightning and by weather.

The white pine was the only softwood a good lumberman would consider. It began to build a nation in 1623 with the construction of the first sawmill, and became our houses and furniture, our matchsticks and window sashes, our figureheads and our meeting halls. It was traded for African slaves who were shipped to the West Indies and sold for sugar and rum.

51

Colonists were forbidden to fell the pines that bore the mark of the King's broad arrow. They were the mast trees, property of the English navy. But the colonists hacked them down anyway as they moved inland, turning forest into farm.

Virgin white pine, soft and orange-colored, cut, it was said, like a knife through pumpkin. Second-growth pine, which is what we see today, is beautiful wood. But it is not the same. It lacks the virtue of age.

By the end of the 1800s, the great stands of white pine had completely disappeared. Maine had been the first to boom and bust. Our buffalo was gone.

Uphill from the land we bought, a tiny cemetery sits behind an iron fence. Most of the stones are old. One records that George A. Bonsey, Company G, Maine Contingent, Heavy Artillery, died in the Battle of Spotsylvania in 1864, the last full year of the Civil War. He was twenty-nine. Spotsylvania was a courthouse town on the way to Fredericksburg. Along its meandering dirt road, Grant and Lee directed their sparring armies. On the last day of battle as the muddy, exhausted soldiers pulled loose from each other, Union artillery reinforcements arrived at noon from Washington. They bedeviled Lee's retreating flank. There were few deaths that day. All was reported relatively quiet at the front. But Private Bonsey, new to battle, died there. Our old white pine could have been no more than ten feet tall in 1864, thin and smooth-barked and softly tasseled. But now, like a gothic vault, it pointed into the sky, exhorting all who saw it where to direct their thoughts.

On its south side, thick dead branches stood out from a deep seam in the bark. The scar, rising halfway up the tree, shaped the trunk like a heart. Seventy years ago — at least — a careless lumberman had dropped another tree against it. The wound healed over, but the tree had been damaged within. Birds used the stout vantage of these branches. On them doves and robins, black throated green warblers, Cooper's and sharp-shinned hawks stopped in turn to case the territory. At night, one of the branches became a hunting platform for an owl.

After arduous soil testing, we were told that the only place we could build was in the clearing, and the only place in the clearing we could build was in the shadow of that pine. It had to come down.

One hundred and fifty feet tall, eleven feet in circumference at the base, and coursed with rot, it might not have fallen for another century. But if it did, or if one of the branches split off in a high wind, it would fall on us.

There was a hum and a sputter, a brief moment when the saw questioned the work it was about to do. The tree shivered. Pollen dusted our shoulders and hair. Then the saw ripped in earnest. The tree leaned. With a sound like a deep gasp, it fell. It bounced once into the clearing. A cloud of pollen obscured it for a moment. When the pollen cleared, the glaucous tassels rose from the limbs, hiding the upper trunk in a soft hedge.

We looked at the woods where it had stood, anticipating the hole the tree would leave. There was no hole — only a gathering of five straight, young pines, their trunks clean two-thirds of the way up, and on the last third, heavy whorls of branch and tassel.

Funny, we hadn't noticed those five trees before.

The Winter Wren

I am looking for the nest of the winter wren. Over the piles of roots and trees around our building site and into the narrow corridors between the pulp logs we have stacked to one side, I am hunting the loose ball of dried mosses and pine needles.

Our newly built house sits in a crater of rubble as if it fell from the sky with force enough to pitch the earth. Clay and rocks lie around it in a gray corona. We were thinking of buying a load of loam and hiring an hour or two of bulldozing time to clean it up. But we don't want to dismantle the nest of the wren. It could be anywhere.

Winter wrens sometimes choose the roots of upturned cedars; there are three near the house. Their roots surge out of the dirt like the arms of giant octopi stunned as they hove up on the crest of a wave. Stones are clenched in the arms. There are crannies and tunnels. There are places to perch, places for lookout. But I don't see the nest.

This species of wren is our smallest songbird — three and a half inches from its bill to its tail — but it sings a loud song. At dawn the song pulses in this clearing above every other noise. The notes — 113 of them at each singing, according to someone's patient count — are sparked by the four o'clock sunrise. They play upon our eyelids like the first sharp points of light.

We have only seen the bird twice. The song is the presence we live with; it makes us uneasy. It is like smelling a baking cake, the eggs and the vanilla and the sugar blending into one sweet smell as they cook, and then not tasting or touching or even seeing a crumb.

We track the bird, following its spinning trill as if we were following footprints. It leads us deeper and deeper into the woods. We have risen with the sun. Sleepily, we stumble over banks of moss and across slow-moving water that seeps from hidden springs. We are drawn to the edge of our property when the song suddenly stops. The wren is probably no more than a foot or so away. We hear the song of another wren, farther off.

"Every one of these damned birds has read *Green Mansions*," Robert growls, half-dressed, feeling watched and foolish.

When fall approaches, the wrens stop singing. They become visible, casual. The parent birds and the young busy themselves in the leaf mold, hunting the last summer insects. When we approach, they call out *tick-tick . . . tick-tick* — a rough, warning sound. Only a few migrating birds linger after the killing frost and into the short, steely days. Before they fly south, the wrens will keep company with someone who comes outside to split wood. Robert had a wren waiting on his boot once as he drove his axe into the heart of a log, exposing a run of carpenter ants. The bird leapt from his toe and danced over the log.

A pair of broad-winged hawks nests in a spruce twenty yards from our house. They turn over the population of our summer woods. We lost the first male robin to arrive in April — a bold, incautious singer. In the pond the feathers of a blue jay that had come to bathe drift idly against the bank. There have been spring litters of red squirrels; their numbers remain constant. The broad-wings see to that.

However, the hawks have missed the garter snake that sleeps in a coil on the clay at the south side of the well on sunny afternoons. And they have ignored the winter wren. Too small to bother with, too fast.

Not only does the wren's voice deceive; so does its nest. The male builds mock nests within his territory and makes his rounds, decoy to decoy, singing his heart out as if each were the real thing.

Yesterday, when Robert started the car, there was a brief, explosive pop. Smoke drooled out of the tailpipe, along with shreds of sphagnum: a decoy nest. In the one where the female hides, the eggs have hatched by now. The five or six young, featherless and as plump as ticks, must be thrusting up their tiny, wizened heads.

Today, the male is building again, this time in the sleeve of Robert's jacket hung in the shed. We see him at last; from the other side of the pond we watch him work. He bounces up the steps, his bill loaded with rootlets and sphagnum and sticks. He flies up into the sleeve and packs everything in. Three trips in five minutes. And between every few trips, he flits into the woods where we can't see him, and he sings.

Years ago, when our cats were young and preferred wild game, one brought us a winter wren. Crouched by a brush pile, she had been hunting voles. Perhaps she thought she had caught one until she felt the feathers on her tongue.

The dead bird rested in my palm, a small, soft windup toy, its tail still propped jauntily aloft, its delicate toes curled. The wren had the richest brown plumage I have ever seen. There was a light in it, a burning orange under-hue.

There will be no loam this summer and no bulldozer. We don't tell anyone that we traded a green lawn for a brown bird's song.

Cait's Coons

Through the open window drifted the odor of sweet thawing dirt from the bare gardens outside. The rain had stopped; the night was silent. Stars had come out. Looming in the yard, the red maple stood black against the cold, dark sky. Even its smallest branches bore dozens of tight pink buds.

"Listen!" whispered Cait. We leaned toward the window.

"Coons," she smiled. She was right. Chittering, high and thin and far away, broke the silence.

"I bet they're yours," said Rob.

"I remember the first day we got them — how cold they were," she said. It was the spring when she was ten.

Infant raccoons had been left at the sanctuary in Ellsworth; Cait had volunteered to raise them. When I set their box on the kitchen floor and Cait drew up the lid, four cubs sprawled in the folds of an old overcoat, listless, thin little raccoons, no more than three weeks old. Their heads were almost as large as their bodies. They had broad foreheads and attenuated, foxlike faces. We lifted them out. The hair of their coats felt dry and coarse; they splayed on the floor, crying in high staccatos.

"How long do you think they've been hungry?" Cait asked as she gathered them into her lap. I had no idea. I didn't even know how they had been found. We heated a bottle of sugar water and another of infant formula, which she offered to each. The cubs pawed at the nipples. They were too big for their mouths, too rubbery, too unlike their mother's teats. For five hours, Cait held the cubs, coaxed them, massaged their stomachs with a damp cloth, and persuaded them to take a little milk. Finally, she fell into a weary sleep.

At midnight, I was walking one of the cubs. The others lay in their

59

box next to Cait, warmed by the hot water bottle that she had wrapped in a towel and by the light we had hung above them. That light, the only one left on in the house, confirmed for me how deep the darkness outside had become. The raccoon wailed at my shoulder; the sound filled up the room and echoed through the vast space outside.

Cait lay on the couch, her face toward the light, her mouth slightly parted, not hearing the bleating of this little raccoon. I tried to feed it, burp it. Nothing stopped the piteous sound. At last, I laid it among its siblings, drew the lamp back over them, and curled up next to my daughter.

When the cries grew fainter, I told myself that the raccoon was being eased out of its misery by the feel of its brothers breathing steadily in a tight knot around it. But I knew differently. The inside of its mouth and the pads of its paws had been too cold. Once, toward morning, I woke to silence, then fell asleep again.

The raccoon was dead. At dawn the three other cubs stirred over its stiff body, begging for milk. Cait wrote the approximate birth date of the cub and the day of its death with a crayon on a cedar shingle. I dug a hole under a white pine where she buried it, wedging her shingle into the dirt for a headstone. Ceremony done, she went back to the living.

The three remaining male cubs slept on their backs, their stomachs distended from the last feeding, as if sleep had come upon them suddenly — a good fairy's spell. As Cait drew off the towel that covered their box, they stretched and peered up at her with blue, unfocused eyes.

The cubs soon learned to take their bottles and drink them dry. Their bodies kept a rhythm like the tides — of fullness and of hunger. Aware of little else, they keyed to Cait's voice the way they must have to their mother's — the way bay water keys to the moon.

Raccoons are not mammals of deep forest like fishers or bobcats. Adult raccoons hunt the deltas where streams empty and thickets, fields, and second-growth woodlots where insects, tubers, and birds' eggs are plentiful and within their reach. Raccoons mate in winter. Females give birth to litters in the spring.

Female raccoons have insatiable appetites in the spring. They need to gain back the weight lost in winter sleep — often up to fifty percent — and their bodies need food to make the rich milk to nurse their cubs. Prying loose old boards to rabbit hutches and hen houses, raccoons devour whatever food they find. They tip garbage cans. They lick up the leavings in hog troughs. Spring is a season when caution is blunted by the sharpness in a raccoon's belly. The mother of our cubs had been shot one night at a farm.

By day, mother raccoons tend to their cubs in the den. That contact is basic to the health of the cubs, as it is to all infant mammals. But in May and in early June, as darkness falls, a mother raccoon will slip away from her sleeping cubs. Pausing at the den's entrance, she will sniff the damp night air and listen to its sounds before she climbs down the tree to hunt.

After a week, the raccoons were stronger. They crawled without toppling. They lay in Cait's lap, chirring, thrusting up their paws to catch at her fingers or any object she might dangle in front of them. "They look like monkey feet," Cait laughed.

It was true, their paws did look like monkey feet, which I suppose means that they look almost human. The black pads of a raccoon's front and back paws are plump and soft. The toes and fingers are long, without the webbing between them that dogs and cats and most other nonhoofed mammals have. Each digit of a raccoon's paw has a freedom of movement almost equal to that of the human hand. But they don't have opposable thumbs. Within the flesh of their front paws, networks of nerve endings help raccoon "hands," especially when wet, read the world like a good book.

Raccoons never trust their nearsighted eyes. As our cubs grew, they would sit on their haunches and listen. Only their glistening noses would move, scenting the air, as their ears cupped stiffly in the direction of a sound. What they knew, they learned through touch and smell and hearing. Sight merely confirmed a good hunch.

We are told that no living thing is exactly like another. Even a blade of grass maintains a staunch singularity. But raccoons are easier to tell apart than blades of grass. Cait named the smallest cub Runty. His face was narrow, and his eyes, close together as in all raccoons, barely spanned the bridge of his snout. He looked cross-eyed. We were surprised to find that even little raccoons develop large Napoleonic complexes. Runty was the pusher, the grabber, the one who threw a fit if he couldn't be first. If he had to wait for his bottle, he jammed his fist into his mouth, sucked at all the knuckles, and screamed. His brother, Benjamin, was a large, strong, but rather diffident raccoon. Gentle and absent-minded, his passion as a cub was to suck on Caitlin's or Aran's chin. He made loud, sloppy sounds, creating a suction strong enough to peel skin. The children, falling back on the floor with Benjamin stuck to their faces, would shriek and try — in vain — to pull him loose.

The third cub Cait named Einstein. ("Although," she confessed, "I'm not too sure he's smart.") Einstein was between the other two in size. A reflective, affectionate cub, he was the only one that seemed to turn over in his mind the option of being a pet for life. His manner was quiet and serious. He believed in taking his time.

Within a month, our upstairs reeked unforgivingly of raccoon. It was time to wean them, time to show them the yard. We moved the cubs to a cage in the shed, and soon after, introduced them to the shallow, sphagnum-filled puddle at the edge of the woods. Thrusting their front paws into the water, they felt along every inch of the bottom, their faces averted, their eyes glazed with rapture. Information poured in at their fingertips, electric with implication.

They cuffed each other, parodying the strut and duck, the swagger and growl of adult raccoons. Waddling to trees, they bolted a foot or so up the trunks, whimpered, and backpedaled down. One day, through the dappled shadows beneath the pines, a venerable hen approached. The hens claim sovereign jurisdiction over the yard and the immediate woods. Clucking her disdain, the hen kept a beady eye on the cubs. Slowly, almost reluctantly, Einstein crouched, drew his head down, and charged. The hen sprang away, then called to her rapacious band. They came running. Step by step, the hens closed in and the raccoons fled to the safety of Cait's lap.

Caitlin fed the cubs Gerber's chicken sticks and bananas, which they immediately accepted, and creamed corn, which they never seemed to like. Weaning was as simple as that. Soon they were eating dog kibble in a pan, softened with diluted milk, and fighting off the chickens. Growling, curling back their lips to show the gleam of their honed canines, the cubs sat in the milky water of the pan, lifting the kibble out with their forepaws and chewing as fast as they could. It never occurred to them to forget the kibble and eat their oppressors. Chickens, as far as they could tell, were nothing like chicken sticks.

Mornings, Cait opened the cage and let the raccoons free. They flopped down the shed steps and followed Cait's progress, a line of furry Slinkies inching across the yard to the pond and the woods beyond. They cried if Cait tried to leave them.

Their surrogate mother and her brother, Aran, spent hours walking the cubs and gathering them up when their courage failed. Daily, the cubs extended the perimeters of their world. Lured by the mystery in the chinks and crannies of a pile of stones, by the sweetness of wild raspberries, or by a patch of summer mud, they hustled away farther and farther from the house.

At two months, wild cubs are led by their mother from the den. The family becomes nomadic, ranging and sleeping and foraging as it goes. Dogs, owls, wildcats, even large hawks are potential predators. The cubs, no larger than cottontail rabbits, waddle behind their mother, who is ferocious in their defense. She refines their natural curiosity, using it to teach them what to eat and how to protect themselves.

Soon our cubs stopped following Cait. Instead, she followed them, finding their footprints in the sand of an old woods road by the well, or once, as she walked down to the marsh, coming upon them suddenly, their forepaws deep in a bed of sphagnum. They, of course, had heard her approach, but greeted her casually. They showed no interest in accompanying her back to the house.

The nesting broad-winged hawks in our woods, the occasional goshawk, the slow-circling eagles — for some reason none of these predators struck at the fuzzy little backs as the cubs shuffled across the yard on their way to the pond to watch green frogs slap into the water.

But one evening the cubs did not return. By nightfall, Cait, Aran, Robert, and I were tripping through the woods, calling. We checked the road, checked the garbage cans. At dawn, I walked the woods again, returning without finding them. Robert sat on the shed steps, sipping coffee.

"Look in the bird feeder," he smiled. Packed tightly inside, the same gray color as the weathered wood, the cubs were breathing evenly, asleep. One paw hung off the feeder's tray. They must have scooted up the dead stump and crawled in just before sunrise. Our raccoons had become nocturnal.

We never did find where they slept in the woods during the day after they outgrew the feeder. They now came to eat under the cover of night, rattling the handle of the kitchen door. When we opened it, they poked their noses into the shaft of kitchen light and whiffled. Bigger each time than we remembered, they shouldered their way in, galloped to the kitchen, splashed into the dog's water bowl, and scraped the leavings from her food bowl as she watched, incredulous, not sure whether to attack or to run.

They were quick, wild. If they decided not to be touched, we couldn't change their minds. But, for a few shelled almonds, they still might let us lift them, and leaning against us on their backs, clutching the almonds like sea otters with clams in their paws, they would chew exultantly as we carried them out. Benjamin weighed twenty-four pounds, and Einstein and Runty were not far behind.

After eating kibble out in the yard, they hoisted their plushy bulks back up the shed steps and lounged on the doormat, idly chewing its loose strands of hemp. Or they lolled on the top steps, gazing out into the dark. If nothing propelled them out into the night, they turned their energy on the shed. Awake, we listened to them roll bottles, drag rubber boots, knock down boxes, and argue over how to rearrange the winter wood. I would storm downstairs, fling open the door, and yell. But I knew I was licked. Their eyes met mine with gleeful innocence as their hands kept busy.

Fall approached; the cubs became ravenous.

"They're costing us the price of a good 'coon coat," Rob grumbled. They learned the location of our bedroom window on the second floor, and when they were hungry again, around midnight, they sat beneath it and cried. Rob and I looked down. The moonlight picked up the white trimming on their ears, their black masks, even the russet between their shoulder blades. The frost glittered on their long guard hairs. When we could stand it no longer, Rob and I staggered down and fed them. As we shivered on the shed steps, they lumbered over to us, leaned against our legs and purred, dreamy with the onset of winter. Eventually, they vanished into the woods, swallowed by the night, moving away over leaves and sticks without a sound.

"Coon dogs!" my neighbor shouted into the phone.

"What do you mean, coon dogs?"

"Listen! They're running your coons over by the creek!"

I laid the receiver down and opened a window. The close, eager yipping broke the night silence like gunfire. I leapt into the car, blaring the horn, and peeled down the drive. An old truck stood on the side of the road, an empty dog cage bolted to its front bumper with the wire door flapping open. A small man holding a rifle stood at woodside, a smile leaking off his face as he watched my car bear down, slam to a stop, and spray the side of his truck with mud. I jumped in front of him.

"Call off your dogs." My chest was heaving. I wasn't thinking.

"We're just stirring up a few coons, Ma'am." I slowed. Think. Think.

The town constable's car appeared at the crest of the hill. He was responding to the blaring of my horn — it's a small town. He drove up, rolled down the window of his car, and let the motor idle. Our neighbor's husband hiked up the road holding a flashlight. Aran had run from the house barefoot. The night rattled with the baying of those dogs.

"I'm Susan Shetterly." I grabbed the man's hand and shook it. "The coons your dogs are chasing are state-licensed." Sounded pretty good. No one else said a word.

"What does that mean, Ma'am?" He withdrew his hand from mine.

"It means that if you kill one, you'll have to answer to the Attorney General. They're legally his. And" — I took a slow, emphatic breath — "he won't like it." I thought everyone would burst out laughing. No one moved.

"The Attorney General? We didn't know the Attorney General kept coons. But we don't want no trouble." He turned and shouted into the woods.

"Hey, Riley. Bring them dogs in."

"What's that?" From the woods.

"They's a lady here says them coons can't be killed. Get the dogs off 'em now!"

"Thank you," I whispered hoarsely.

"Well, I sure appreciate you telling us. As I said, we don't want no trouble." We shook hands all around as Riley appeared dragging three frenetic, salivating blue ticks. He stuffed them into the cage. The truck eased off the shoulder and puttered up the road.

The constable shifted into first. He smiled. "The Attorney General can rest easy tonight, God bless him." And he drove away.

The first snow fell. The cubs disappeared. Raccoons, however, are not true hibernators. One or another awoke on November nights when the temperature rose, and jiggled the handle of the kitchen door. I pulled on my boots and took out a food pan as Cait pressed her face against the icy window glass and called.

We had read that the first winter sleep turns a male raccoon wild. It is true. They are free of us — more so, I suspect, than we are of them.

"It must be Einstein," Cait decided as she listened to the chittering that spring evening. "He always liked to stay close to home."

Farm Pond

Five years ago, we hired a neighbor to dig us a farm pond. He drove his backhoe over our field into the bog and stopped in front of a stream, an icy thread of water that wound silently between sphagnum-covered stones. A hungry roar and a belch of diesel breath rose out of the machine. Tilting forward, it began to feed on the ferns and roots and stones and the sour accumulations of swamp maple leaves.

Our two children stood at the periphery of his art, next to a white plastic bucket that held the stream's entire population of green frogs. All seven had been gathered that morning and now flopped against the bucket's side, impatient for release. Morning and afternoon, as the two children watched, our neighbor sculpted an oblong hollow.

At sunset, he drove away. The air hushed and cleared. Tire ruts receded over the field, and we were left beside a sleek, gray crater, 30 by 40 feet, encircled by a high, uneven rim of muck. We lifted the green frogs out of the bucket. When they saw what had happened to their sylvan home, they crouched in the devastation and stared.

That night it rained. The crater took in water, mixing with it an unsinkable mist of clay. It rained for a week. The hole slowly filled.

When the sun emerged, the stream had already fought its way back. It poured a fan of pristine water, pushing the suspended clay over the far rim. The pond cleared. The green frogs, garish against the pond's monotone, swam incautiously from bank to bank or floated leisurely, their legs spread wide. On its routine trip from one pond to another, a bittern flew across our span of new water, veered, and came down. We could see it from the garden as it stood on the bank, head and neck thrust skyward, a perfect imitation of a cattail stem. There was nothing nearby but mud and a few green frogs. The bittern glanced down. It turned its head in the windless air, furtively surveying its lonely position. It was the only cattail stem. With a squawk of enlight-enment, it flapped up and over the trees.

We took shovels, and careful not to set off a maelstrom of clay, we smoothed back the banks and scattered lime and grass seed and hay over them. That fall, redwings landed in flocks and ate the seed. The surviving frogs dug into the clay against the coming cold. One clear December night, we built a fire on the snowbank and skated our ellipse of ice.

First to rise the next spring after the snow melt were the cinnamon ferns. From their root knots, which the backhoe had buried, they surfaced with such force that their green fists left fault lines in the clay. A mesh of algae settled over the pond bed. One bone-cold, sunny April afternoon, a harsh cacophony drifted up to the house.

Mallards on the pond! But the pond's surface was bare. No sound of liftoff. No wake. Our daughter walked to the bank.

"There's a stripy pink frog lying on the bottom," she called back.

"Frogs don't quack," we told her.

But they do. From a second-story window, we could see more than sixty of them, flopping on top of each other and bubbling. They were wood frogs. Crawling out of their winter niches into the aching cold, they had the water to themselves. All day long we heard their quack-ing. But when we approached for a closer look, our footfalls carried and they dove. The next morning, floating twigs were braceleted with loose, gelatinous bands of eggs. The frogs stayed for about a week, then disappeared back to the leaf mold and punky logs of the forest floor.

Other egg masses, gray and rubbery, clung in groups to sticks in deeper water. At night, by the beam of a flashlight, we found spotted salamanders wandering the bottom mud as if it were a wide Galapagos.

As soon as the eggs hatched, predacious insects appeared. Like the frogs and salamanders, somehow they knew the pond was here. They came in the dark. Heavy-bodied water beetles droned over the field on diaphanous wings, landing with tiny thuds at the pond. Laboriously, they folded their wings away under brittle wing covers and waded into the night water, their silvery pockets of air catching in the moon's light.

The pond still looked like a crater. The bank bore small, erosive scars. But the arrival of beetles and bugs and flies changed its character. We lay on the hard banks as if on safari, looking down.

There were thousands of tiny polliwogs. They hung to sticks and swarmed over the vacated jelly masses, their rasping teeth cleaning the detritus from everything they touched. They had a rhythm of their own apart from the constant eating: wiggle, pause, wiggle. The pauses were long and the wiggles weak.

A dragonfly larva clung to a slender weed and, with goggle eyes, peered into the murk and the milling polliwogs. It was in no hurry. Beneath its mouth folded an impressive jaw that is at once arm and claw and tooth. The larva sprinted into the herd. With a slow, ecstatic pulsing, it rose, a polliwog thumping in its mouth. Letting the tip of its abdomen pierce the surface of the water, it hung head down and fed.

Backswimmers, whirligigs, and predacious diving beetles all hunt in their own style. And like the birds of the South American jungle canopy that choose branches at a specific height to live in, these insect species prefer water at a certain depth.

The whirligigs swim at the surface in erratic schools, their two pairs of eyes searching simultaneously for enemies above and prey below. Backswimmers slant toward the pond bed, but the plastrons of air stuck to their abdominal hairs carry them up. They row against buoyancy. The diving beetle is not as nervous as the all-seeing whirligig, nor as flailing as the backswimmer. An insect of sober purpose, it examines the underside of a leaf, weaving itself methodically between decomposing sticks and weeds.

By the summer of the second year, tree swallows nesting in a box by the garden glided over the pond at evening. September mornings, a solitary sandpiper hunted where the water brimmed. We threw wild seeds and weeds, gathered from other, larger ponds, along the shore and into the water.

Another spring came with striders skating the first open water and a few minnows that our son had released the year before miraculously thawed out and swimming. When it was warm enough, bladderwort as fine as green lace floated mid-water. Blue-winged teal flew in and out of the pond, leaving gently spreading wakes.

It is the fifth summer. I walk over the raccoon prints in the sandy delta where the stream feeds the deeper water. There are narrow clefts from the hooves of a young deer. I count green frogs. Wading through the reeds and the thigh-high ferns at the far side, I am almost certain that the tall green stalks in the pond's center are young cattails.

This reminds me of something. I look at the lush banks, the clear and busy water, the trees playing with shadow, and the sun above them. And then I know. It reminds me of the bog.

Halcyon Days

At low tide, a belted kingfisher flapped across the bay's flat sheen. Its voice, like a string of cans tied to a running dog, clattered behind it.

The bird swung onto a telephone line. It sat tipped slightly forward, focusing on the water running under the culvert. For a long time it waited. Then the wings spread and tucked. The bird tilted, fell, pierced the surface, and disappeared in a small explosion of spray.

The force that bore it down brought it up. In an easy arc it resumed its perch, a fish flapping in its beak. Methodically, almost absent-mindedly, the kingfisher slapped the writhing silverside against the telephone line, shook it, and ran the fish's bruised length back and forth. Satisfied at last that what remained was palatable, the bird grasped its catch head first and swallowed.

It reminded me of the kingfisher I had raised the summer before, which had been brought to the sanctuary by some children. I wondered if mine had survived, as this one had, to migrate back to the open water.

The nestling kingfisher sat on a towel in my car, listless, withdrawn, and giving off an aroma of ripe fish. It resembled a lizard. As it crouched in the cardboard box, I would not have been surprised had it dashed up the side and whipped under the driver's seat. Instead, with large, blank eyes, it returned my gaze, swaying slightly to the car's rhythm.

It must have been nearly two weeks out of the egg, for kingfishers are naked and blind at birth. This bird was covered with feathers furled in protective sheaths. Each sheath looked like a gray-blue straw protruding from the flesh. To the touch, it was a warm and oily stubble.

To simulate a nesting chamber, we propped a five-gallon can at an angle in a wooden barrel and draped a towel over it. Cait and Aran

71

smoothed a lining of newspapers and tissues against the can's interior. When lowered into it, the bird skittered toward the dark.

The kingfisher refused food. By nightfall, I had force-fed it haddock strips and found a smooth, white pouch, like a purse lined in satin, at the base of its lower mandible. It slept that night with its purse full.

The species name for this kingfisher comes from the word "halcyon." Greek legend has it that the birds nest on the sea at the winter solstice. Gods of water and of wind calm the surface; the sea lies like a sheet beneath the young birds and does not rise into waves until they fledge and fly away. Thus, our halcyon days: a brief time of peace.

Belted kingfishers return to Maine as soon as the bays and lakes unlock. For most of the year they are solitary birds, jealous of their claim to a stretch of water and the branches extending over it. But in spring they pair and dig a nesting chamber into a bank a few feet from the summit. Radiantly white, the eggs rest in the nursery.

Most of the fish taken by kingfishers are considered "trash fish" by men: minnows, suckers, menhaden, and other common species of our shallow waters. To avoid being hooked by a dorsal spine, the bird swallows its catch head first, allowing the fins to fold back naturally. A hungry kingfisher will eat almost anything if fish are scarce. It hunts frogs, mice, small birds, and even snakes. More than one kingfisher has been found with its bill in the grip of a freshwater clam, helpless for as long as the embattled mollusk holds.

Early the next morning, a hard rattle woke me. It sounded as if something metal were slowly bending over, ripping, and falling away. When I reached the bird room and lifted the towel, a great factory of sound rose from the five-gallon can.

I speared a strip of fish with a blunt stick, dipped it into a mix of vitamins and calcium, and slowly lowered it. The bird charged, wrestled the fish from the tip, the noise reeling and heaving. Rushing to the interior of the can, the kingfisher shielded the food with its wings and gulped it down. Back up at a run, the voice less loud this time but still strident, the bird ripped another strip from the stick and plunged to the bottom. Finally, the noise petered out. The bird began to wag its tail as if dancing, lifted it, squirted a chalky stream against the side of the can, then shuffled back down, turned around on the tissue like a sleepy dog, and closed its eyes.

This peculiar feeding behavior, an adaptation for living in the dark with a group of hungry siblings, is triggered in the wild by the patter of a parent's feet down the tunnel. I watched the bird settle — halcyon, my foot. I wondered how many ancient Greeks ever raised one.

The kingfisher learned my voice. It matched and overpowered mine with its own. But it never imprinted, never became tame.

Kingfishers are shaped for the shallow dive. The large head and heavy bill draw the fulcrum of the body forward. The wings are rounded for quick, precise flight. This is one of the few North American bird species in which the female is more colorful than the male. A stain of rust across her chest breaks up the subtle markings of blue and white. Our kingfisher was female.

When lifting the bird to change the towels, we found that her warm gut hung, bowl-shaped, down to her tiny feet. The paunch is common in baby birds that fledge on hard surfaces without the support of a nest wall. Until she matured, her belly would relieve the growing legs of her full weight.

On her heels were thick, temporary pads that protected her joints from scuffing. The three front toes of a kingfisher's foot are partially fused. The feet look astonishingly pink and shiny, as if they belong to someone very old who has always worn carpet slippers. In sleep, her head flopped forward and her wings splayed. I never drew away the towel from the can and found her like this without a sudden spasm of fear. She looked as if she had died.

Two weeks after her arrival, the kingfisher's feather sheaths split and her body contours softened. She began to fly out of the can. I collected polliwogs in a baking pan and placed the kingfisher on the rim.

She screamed to be fed. With a cold eye for her life ahead, I refused. She began to howl, her head up and her throat pulsing with the sound. Then she stopped, looked around the floor, spotted our robin in leg braces pulling itself along, and made a dash for it. The little bird turned to see the wide, white mouth, yipped, and scrambled for the far side of the table. I placed the kingfisher back on the pan.

Reaching into the water, she gingerly lifted a polliwog by the tip of its tail. She held it pensively. The way it struggled seemed to jog her instinct, for she began to whack it against the metal sides. When she had finished, there was nothing left but gray slime. She'd overdone it. After a few more tries, she turned into a dead-eye polliwog hunter.

I carried her to the pond and settled her on a limb over the water. She balanced with ponderous care. As parent kingfishers do, I stunned minnows and dropped them before her. She watched them, turning her head from side to side, then bolted into the woods. Sitting on a rock, she listened as I waded through sphagnum, drew back a clump of ferns, and leaned toward her. As my hand dropped over her back, she slid off the rock and into the brush. I crashed and slipped behind her.

Day after day we repeated this scene with only minor variations. Perhaps she learned something about survival or perhaps she simply developed a lifelong distaste for minnows. I learned I must set her free.

One morning I put her in a box and drove to West Bay Pond, a wide spread of water descending over rocks to tannic pools, then to a lake that empties into the bay. I opened the box and let her fly. She dashed out across the expanse with that wonderful flip of an adult kingfisher. And she celebrated with a rattling call. I knew that she would land somewhere in the trees on the far bank. I hoped that hunger would bring her to the water and a combination of instinct and lessons would tell her what to do.

Quiet settled over the water. My halcyon days were over.

SUMMER

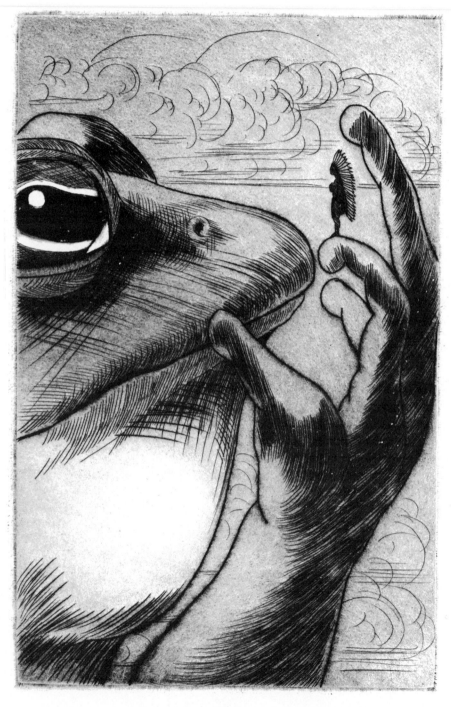

The Frog

It gazes through the years, the irises of its eyes golden, its expression somber, watchful. Sometimes at night, here in Maine, I see that wet face grown the size of the sky, its skin shining all over with stars. And sometimes I set my mind to remember the time of the frog.

When we visited the farm all those years ago, we slept in the attic, under the raw eaves. Even when I was very young, I remember how it felt for us to be lined up on army cots beneath the ridgepole of a tin roof, my sister, Maggie, my father, my mother, and me. We were refugees, I thought, or pilgrims or pioneers. If we visited in the fall, I could see frost out the window, twinkling in a broad swath over the cow pasture, and the cows moving through the night, as black as bears.

My father never did like the farm in Flemington, New Jersey, where my godmother lived. My mother expressed such exuberant delight my sister and I were suspicious. But Maggie and I loved it.

Naomi was my godmother. By the time I knew her, she had become a farmer's wife. She wore Ralph's work pants held up by a belt, and men's work shirts rolled to the elbows. Her skin was pale, fine-looking. Her arms were plump and comfortable.

Her straight brown hair was shaved at the back like a boy's, exposing the unadorned neck. It fell in bangs on her forehead, and in two angular flaps at her ears — a cut thirty-five years out of date. Curious, because there was nothing like a flapper about Naomi, nothing giddy or carefree. And if she was brave, which I imagine she was, it wasn't a reckless bravery.

Naomi was shy. Her voice was a slight, cool voice. After graduating from Wellesley, Naomi had been tutor to a prince's children in Siam. She had lived in exotic splendor. I tried to visualize her as Anna, throwing out her arms to the black-haired, giggling children and teach-

77

ing them how to whistle. But she didn't fit. Too alone by nature. Too shy.

In her composed and unobtrusive manner, Naomi *was* the farm. But she kept unfarmlike signs. Her leather-bound books with their titles stamped in gold, for instance, and her symphonies issuing from the dim utilitarian living room. That music rolled out as if the living room were a cavern, or some deep recess of the heart. As a child, I would come upon Naomi standing at the kitchen table or out in the yard, her hands checked at their task. I was startled by the force of her silence. She was listening.

Ralph's parents lived on the farm behind, up a dirt road. Ralph was shy, too, but not with children. He took my sister and me to gather eggs out of the nest boxes, pushing the warm-bellied hens up so our hands could slip under, our fingers searching out the shape of an egg. He drove us in the tractor. He taught us how to fold a slice of bacon to a hook so it wouldn't slough off, and how to let it bump along with the current into muddy catfish lairs, its flaccid greasiness vanishing into the silt. He sat me on the kitchen table and pulled out my loose tooth with a pair of pliers. I adored him for it. He made ice cream with the top milk from the cows. He taught me how to paddle a canoe.

I was ten when I started going to the farm alone from our house on the Connecticut shore. Rainy days that summer, I crawled under the blankets of my cot after lunch and read by the light of the only window. The drops thrummed on the tin roof above me like a spill of nails. The window looked out on the cow pasture and the stream, which turned silver those afternoons as the cows ambled, soaked and shiny, over the soggy humps of grass.

One by one, I worked down a board and cinder block shelf of "National Geographics" arranged in order from April 1940. Because I was ten and flat-chested and anxious, I studied the breasts the most. Some sagged like sacks full of stones. Some hung like empty socks. Some were even tattooed down to the mahogany nipples as if the skin of those women were carved bark. The women were as dark as trees. I studied lions rending the neck of a terrified giraffe. And lions gnawing casually on the ribs of a glazed-eyed antelope. I studied a girl, a few years older than I was, with silver rings on her neck, her neck stretching up like the giraffe's. Then I turned back to the breasts.

Sunny afternoons, Ralph sent me to his parents' springhouse for the milk pail. The dust of the road stuck between my toes and rose up my legs as Terry, the farm whippet, snuffled through the undergrowth. The Osage orange trees arched above us and, occasionally, a green, pock-marked fruit would smack into the dirt and send up the dust like a puff of signal smoke. The glossy-leafed trees filtered the sunlight onto the road and made dancing shadows over it. I thought of Indians. I walked as I imagined they must have, dusty and loose-limbed, cautious, ready for any danger.

When Terry and I stopped at the door of the springhouse, I lifted the string and entered into that cold, astringent shade. He lay down on a patch of grass outside. The door swung shut. The milk pail stood on a bridge of slippery boards over the water. As I worked my way across the boards, they shivered. Some of the milk sloshed out of the pail and dripped into the water.

From the watercress, curled around the perimeters of the spring, a frog nosed up suddenly, and waited. I saw its white throat patch pulse and glisten as it breathed. Its gold-flecked eyes stared. Slowly, heavily, hunched on the boards, I splashed the dust off my feet and legs. I picked up a piece of cress and shook it and chewed it as the frog watched.

"The time has come to tell you," I intoned, leaning out over the boards toward the frog's face. It sat as if waiting, unafraid.

"I am Great White Eagle Feather!" I leaned out even farther. My mouth was just a few inches from the frog's mouth.

"I speak the language of the animals."

The Bats of Summers Past

My mother believed that she was graced with country wisdom. For example, she taught us that mosquitoes retreat from light. On camping trips to freshwater lakes on Cape Cod, she would hand my sister and me our flashlights at dusk. We lay in our sleeping bags on those shores, coning our lights into the darkness as if we were tracking German bombers. A few thousand mosquitoes ignored the lights. The rest didn't dare.

My mother also taught us that bats crave human hair. She had long Irish hair. By day, she wore it in a bun. But when she let it down at night, it radiated from her head and she looked as if the ghosts of her ancestors, sent wandering the back roads of County Mayo, barefoot and homeless during a famine, possessed her still.

I remember the summer I learned that the belief she held in the perfidy of bats was as absolute as her faith in a forgiving God. I was nine. We lived in an old Connecticut house and she was putting me to bed with a story. A summer breeze stirred the curtains. The night was muggy. A whisper of air from the window only shifted the heaviness in the room as we lay under a sheet on my bed. Her voice slowed as she read, and the words slurred ever so slightly. My eyes closed. Suddenly, she flung the sheet aside.

"A bat!" she shrieked. The springs under the mattress heaved in her wake. She dove out of my bedroom, slamming the door behind.

In a crisis a child's mind does not question the propriety of a parent's behavior. A child, like an adult, mobilizes for survival. I retrieved the sheet. I drew it over my head and placed my hands above my nose and mouth in a prayer position to give me a space to breathe. The bat grazed the sheet. My skin prickled. I could hear it tapping at the corners of the room.

"Don't move a muscle!" My father flung open the door. He was swinging a tennis racket. It hit my desk. I heard him lunge to catch the lamp. He cursed, swung, and cursed again. Then I heard the connection — the *boing* which comes from the racket's center when all the cat gut evenly reverberates. My father lobbed the bat out the window.

Myotis lucifugus, "the one who flees the light," is an appropriate name for the bat that exited with such dispatch. It must have been returning to the eaves after hunting insects and missed its entry to the attic. This species, which we call the little brown bat, had been darting back and forth in the dark for almost forty million years before human creatures flailed their first cudgels.

I don't remember if my sister or I ever questioned what bats were, where they went in winter, or how they caught their food. To us, bats were creatures to poke at, tedious animals during the day. But by night they flew above our heads, mad for human hair.

Bats have not changed much since they evolved from shrewlike animals, voracious hunters of the forest floor. There are lots of gliders, but bats are the only mammals to fly. As a child, I remember being fascinated by how they looked. Their fur was disheveled, their eyes tiny. From their back toes, wisps of hair stood up. Their nails were tapered and curved.

The wings of a little brown bat are a double layer of skin, tautly stretched between the elongated four fingers of the front paws and down the sides of its body to the tail. The fifth finger, or thumb, is a small, free hook. The interfemoral membrane, a leaf-shaped flap of skin attached to the back feet, runs to the tip of the tail. The knees of these bats bend in reverse of ours. By kicking the knees back and the feet forward, little browns scoop up insects into that pouch. They can also catch insects in their mouths or in either wing, like infielders lunging after line drives.

There are two suborders of bats. Those called flying foxes (now considered by some to be of primate origin) have large eyes that afford them the nighttime vision of nonflying mammals. They are strictly visual bats, feeding on fruit and flower nectar in the tropics. The others, such as the little brown, live in temperate climates. With 20/400 vision, they see only hazily. They orient themselves by hearing rather than by sight, and their prey is the night-flying insect.

Little brown bats are colonial. Year after year, pregnant females return to their traditional maternity wards — the attics, belfries, and cabins of our towns — to bear and raise their young. Our house was obviously an ancestral home of the first order. That large and rambling building was surrounded by two barns, a long strip of woods, and across the road, a stream into which weeping willows trailed their yellow branches. Slow and dark and clean, the water hid an occasional trout, as well as minnows and eels. The house had been there for a century and a half — time enough for generations of humans *and* bats. Its attic was a series of dusty, cramped rooms with small-paned windows that collected the dry, honey-colored bodies of trapped insects on their sills. It had a costume box. Old books. And, in summer, it had bats. They lived behind the plaster, close to the eaves.

Periodically, my father hired an exterminator. We left on vacation and the attic was pumped full of cyanide gas. Upon return, we lived in the arch silence of our neighbors across the yard; most of our bats had escaped in one black cloud and scrambled under their eaves. Come fall, bats left their roosts on the Connecticut shore and migrated inland to winter caves. Some traveled more than two hundred miles to northern caves, into the face of the advancing cold. After their departure, all would be neighborly again.

In the dark hibernation caverns, various species congregate. You can run your hand along them as if you were stroking the back of a large, passive beast. The bats undulate in waves as your hand draws across them.

A bat hanging by its hind feet to the wall of a cave has a body temperature not much above the temperature of the air. Its heartbeat is slow and faint. Unlike most small, active mammals, bats have prodigious life spans. A little brown can live for twenty-five years. When hunting, a bat's metabolism is as rapid as a short-tailed shrew's, whose life expectancy is no more than a year or two. Hibernation and the rest period between feedings lower a bat's average metabolism. These periods of intense activity interspersed with torpor grant them their longevity.

Bats usually mate in the fall. In the cold caves, drowsy with the onset of hibernation, their coats pearled with moisture, two bats hang to the wall by their hind feet, clamped together, and as one, drift off to sleep. The low temperature of the female prevents ovulation. But the sperm lives inside her, the egg ready, until she stirs and begins her migration to the nursery — a sleeping beauty awakened not by the kiss but by the disengagement.

When little browns disperse from their winter caves, the males become errants, traveling and sleeping where they will. The females head for the nurseries where they were born. A nursery may hold a thousand female bats, their pregnancies accelerated by the heat of those summer attics.

Little brown bats have a surprisingly long gestation period for animals so small: sixty days, as opposed to twenty-one for mice and voles. At birth, the baby bat is well developed. As the time of parturition nears, the female little brown reverses her customary resting position and hooks to the ceiling by her thumbs. She curves up her tail, creating a pliant cradle into which the baby drops. Its weight is almost a quarter of her own, a little under two grams. Clawing free of the placenta, it struggles through her fur. The incurved teeth lock around a nipple. Its thumbs and feet grip tight. Despite its weight, the mother bat can carry the infant for a few days while she hunts. Later, when the weight increases, she leaves the baby hanging in the nursery.

In Connecticut, August heat blistered what was left of the paint on our attic floor. The bat population behind the falling plaster doubled. During the day, mothers and young and some returned adult males flopped down the stairwell and bunched against the attic door, searching, perhaps, for a breath of fresh air.

One afternoon my mother called me in from the barn across the road. I had been lying in the hayloft reading *Tom Sawyer* and watching the swallows, already too old for their nests, rocketing from the wide doorway of the barn out the window at the other end, and up in spirals into the sky. An old friend of my mother's from New York was visiting with her daughter. The girl, in Mary Janes and a starched pinafore over her summer print, sat on the sofa. The afternoon light fell on her shoulders like a watercolor wash. She was pale and fat and soft, a year or two older than I. When we were introduced, she eyed me mistrustfully and shook her brown banana curls. Dutifully, I asked if she'd like to play.

First, I said, we have to get some sticks. I led her to the woods and snapped off two alder branches. As I peeled back the bark with my fingers, I knew that although she gave no indication, she was impressed. Patiently, I explained to her that the point of the game was to get a bat to bite the stick and hold on as we lifted it. The winner was the one who kept a bat up in the air the longest.

When I opened the attic door, she drew back. The bats squeaked and flapped about on their rubbery-looking wings. When it is as hot as it was that day, bats are restless and irritable. Perhaps they suspected we were about to play that same old game again. Their wrinkled faces screwed up. They threatened us with rows of spiked teeth. I offered my stick to the most churlish on the stairs. At first, it refused. But after a few prods, it got into the spirit of things and bit down hard on the alder branch. I lifted it. Not high — just a foot above the others — and began to count. It dropped back into the heap at "five."

"Now it's your turn," I challenged. But she had left. Her stick was lying on the floor.

The nights of deep summer in Connecticut started, or so it seemed when I was a child, as never-ending evenings. A sweet damp spread up from the frog pond. The air took forever to lose its light. My father, back from New York, would pull out his arthritic aluminum chaise, fiddle with its uncompromising joints, and finally sink back, the ice clinking in his drink. One by one, bats dropped from the eaves of our house. They fluttered past the second story, spread their wings, and set their courses over the lawn and the hedges and the frog pond in erratic tilted parabolas. Their voices scraped like hinges of old, sagging pasture gates, opened to let the cows come home.

My sister and I lay on our backs in the grass watching. We didn't know then — although almost everybody knows now — that the occasional sounds we heard from the hunting animals above us were only the desultory comments of bat to bat. The real noise was fracturing the thick air in waves so far above our ability to hear that we mistook it for silence.

No one knows all the answers to how echolocation works, although we have learned that it is the ability to throw the voice precisely, to have it ricochet off a target. From that bounce, the bat obtains information on the size, direction, and speed of its prey. Shrews, whales, porpoises, and some birds use echolocation to varying degrees. But no other animal has developed it to the art of the bat. The high-frequency sounds are pulses rather than a continual noise. Little brown bats throw their voices in a rat-a-tat-tat. Each pulse takes less than one two-hundredth of a second. The blast of the pulse is tremendous — twice what it would be for us if we pounded away at a city pavement with a pneumatic drill. At the fraction of a second in which the sound is emitted, the muscles of the bat's middle ear contract, preventing self-inflicted deafness. In the next instant, the ears open.

Three weeks after their birth, little brown bats are ready to fly. Flying and hunting by echolocation are inherited instincts. But bats must learn how to maneuver, how to hone their voices and interpret the echoes.

Little brown bats are selective feeders, taking mosquitoes, midges, ichneumon wasps, and some moths. Each can average five hundred insects an hour. After the hunt, they retire to digest their food, fatter than when they emerged from the eaves by almost thirteen percent. Before dawn, they hunt again.

Some night-flying insects, in response to echolocation, have developed strategies against it. Some are able to hear the high-frequency hunting pulse. If you stand under a lamppost on a summer night when moths are swarming in a halo around it, rattle your car keys. A few of the moths will plunge to the ground. Others will zigzag their flight patterns. And others have developed jamming techniques that scramble a bat's vocal pulses and disrupt the echoes. When fully aroused and in good health, bats perceive the world around them with such accuracy that they can fly under and over wires almost invisible to the human eye. Had my mother known this, she might have respected the skill the bats employed to stay free of her hair.

My mother taught me more than survival skills. She taught me that justice comes, that the mills grind fine. That same summer she abandoned me to a bat, on a Sunday morning she dressed early for church. As usual, she looked impeccable — casual, but everything in place. I had planned to go fishing. The thought of trading the quick dip and disappearance of a bobber and the willowed silence of the stream bank for the parched smell of incense and endless hymns was almost more than I could bear.

As I came downstairs, reluctant in a summer dress, she was standing on the flagstone terrace. She was leaning forward somewhat, her body at attention, the toes of her patent leather heels turned out. Her left hand was cocked to her ear.

"Susie," she called gaily to me, "I hear the most interesting bird!"

And then I saw it. One of her heels had skewered the wing of a bat. It lay at her foot, squealing. I felt a stab of hysterical joy. But I decided to approach her calmly.

"Do you hear it?" she asked, turning to me. Incredibly, she did not look down. Her face was serene and expectant as her eyes met mine.

"Yes," I said, and smiled up at her. "You are standing on a bat."

She shot into the air. Her hair seemed to leap from her head as if it had a mind of its own. A hairpin clinked to the flagstones. A shoe rolled off the terrace and the kitchen door slammed behind her.

Quietly, I scooped the weary bat into her shoe and shook it out under a bush. It crawled into the shadows. I slipped upstairs, changed into my shorts and T-shirt, found my fishing pole in the garage, and headed for the stream.

The Grand Marsh

The white bird rose from the pool and glided over the backs of the four other common egrets — uncommon sights on this down east marsh. I followed it with my binoculars. I lay behind a patch of field grass in front of a cracked cement wall, part of the cellar hole of an abandoned house. The ground was bumpy with mole runs.

Suddenly, a dark wing fanned in front of my glasses. A bald eagle shot in under the flying egret. I saw the other waders skitter aside. The eagle twisted; the egret above it beat wildly. The big bird was cutting it off from the marsh, forcing it up.

"No!" I shouted. I was too far away. A hoarse, tight cry rose out of the egret's throat. I watched its neck stretch out, its legs stiffen, its body heave with effort and fear. The huge bird guided it like a sheep dog cutting off one sheep from the herd. The egret will crash down somewhere, I thought, when the eagle, in one swift gesture, circles on top and hits it — just hard enough to knock it out of the air. They were only two dots now, erratic movements in the blue emptying sky.

Back at the marsh pool, the other waders busily fed. Nothing had happened. Nothing at all.

I've spent more time than I like to admit in front of this cellar hole, lying on the spongy ground. No one else I know bothers about this marsh unless it is duck hunting season. Once, the Gouldsboro Grand Marsh was essential to the people of Prospect Harbor. It grew the grasses that ripened into salt hay in the July heat. Every precious foot of it was bound into a family lot and passed down from one generation to the next. Draft horses lugged recalcitrant wagons across the mud and stood flicking their tails against hordes of marsh mosquitoes and salt flies as men and boys scythed the hay and piled it into the wagons for winter.

At the mouth of the bay, the townspeople had built a dike to keep the spring tides out. The dike is a ruined spine now; whole sections of it have fallen away. Wild celery and seaside goldenrod root on its spent slopes. Tides have enlarged the channels that cut through the marsh. The channels are sleek and dangerous places for a bear or a dog or a deer or me. But wading birds, whose feet distribute their small weights so evenly they could almost walk on water, leave only footprints in that precarious ooze.

The first time I stepped out of the tree line onto the marsh, and the Canada geese, the black duck, the green-winged teal, and the waders burst from it, turned, and headed out to sea, I was surprised by the long stretch of grasses. It was larger than I had imagined — almost a prairie expanse. One day, I walked the entire circumference, one hundred and fifty acres, past the apple trees with the bear spoor beneath, past the road under which the sweet marsh gullies into the salt, past the rise where poplars and beeches rustle their dry leaves in the hot wind.

I came to a channel. I followed it, hoping for a span that I could jump. It was low tide and the greater yellowlegs, feeding within, shrieked their three-note warnings one after another like a bunch of alarm clocks set at half-minute intervals. They wouldn't let me be here without insisting that every other animal on the marsh know it; that's why some people call them tattlers. As soon as one of their alarms went off, a flock of plovers or semipalmated or least sandpipers would snap into the air, make that circle around the circumference, and as one flashing silver-edged bird, disappear over the bay.

I had to cross it. There was no other way. I chose a spot with as much gravel as mud, for I guessed that gravel indicated a solidity that might bear my weight.

"You never want to see someone pulled from the water," a warden told me once. "It's what them snails and crabs do. It's ugly." A green crab scooted past my boot. I remembered that two clam diggers, a year or so before, were caught in a mud channel in a town nearby; their bodies were sucked into the bay when the tide shifted. You wouldn't want to see them, but, having heard that, you imagine.

The tattlers had flown. All about me rose a deafening chorus of brown crickets hidden in the grasses, scraping their hosannas as I sank into the mud. Quickly it took my boot. I slammed my hand down, grabbed the boot, and pulled as the other foot went in. The next step brought the mud to my knees. I lay flat, after throwing the binoculars into the grass above and ahead of me, and laughing a little because the crickets around my glasses stopped singing so suddenly it was as if I'd flicked out a light. As I crawled forward, I could hear them tune up again, cautiously at first, then with renewed confidence.

This was the way to do it; I swam the mud. I reached out and gripped some spartina grass and hauled myself up to the crickets. I rolled over on my back and closed my eyes and let the sun bake the gray mud dry. Next to me, the water in the channel whispered as it began to rise. A northern harrier — a young, copper-breasted hawk — flew over, its shadow falling on my eyelids so that I opened them to its rocking flight, struck by the passion I felt watching it. I thought I had never seen anything quite so fine as that hawk.

The mud crumbled off my shirt as I sat up. Next to me was the shallowest pool, a skim of water with minnows streaking through it and the small, intensely colored glasswort plants glowing around it like votive candles. The spartinas — the salt grasses — smelled sweet and clean. Some were rusty and brown, and lay in soft whorls under me as if they had been pressed down by the warm bodies of deer.

Two black-bellied plovers stood in silhouette on the worn ridges of the old dike. Sentinels, they guarded the flock feeding below them. There were hundreds of birds, despite my presence, darting, feeding, running, rushing from pool to pool. They were the wind birds that roiled away in tight flocks from the far north weeks ago. They would travel farther before the snow fell here, some to the southern shores of Argentina. What a chance — this being alive.

There are probably more lives on the marsh now, feeding and gathering, than there were when every boy and man in town, and every horse that could pull, tramped out to fight the flies and cut the hay. As I walked back to my car by the cellar hole, I stopped to watch an ancient king step into a pool. Like Olivier, playing the last days of Lear, this bird moved brokenly, its spirit tense, hot, kindling at its own narrow flesh and bone. The great blue heron gazed deeply into the pool. One more impossibly slow step ahead. The water accepted the foot and the leg without a ripple. Then the head whapped down. It cleaved the pool in two. The heron plucked out a fish. With a writhing toss of the long neck, it flipped its catch, opened, and closed. Then the neck cramped down upon the shoulders. The bird lifted one stick-thin fractured-looking leg, balanced, and stepped forward ever so slowly, again.

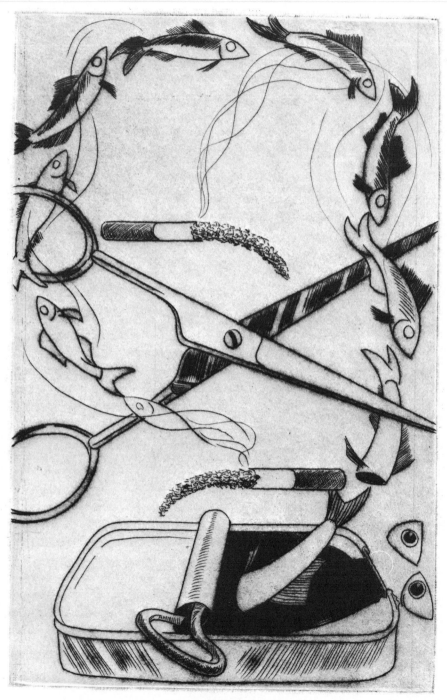

Factory Days

Two months after we moved onto our land, we ran out of money. For some reason, this astonished us. It wasn't that we didn't have enough for a winter's trip to Florida or a second car; we didn't have enough for a comb or a bottle of cooking oil. Laying aside my copy of Helen and Scott Nearing's *Living the Good Life*, I took a job at the local canning factory.

When there were fish to cut, the factory whistle blew. If the fish came from Canada or southern Maine and not by boat, we always knew beforehand, because the factory trucks hurled themselves down the Pond Road in the dark. The Pond Road bears a certain resemblance to a subway tunnel. The trees on either side of it grow up onto the shoulder, and there isn't a curve in it.

Nothing hits this road like a truck with a sloshing belly of fish. It is as if the driver knows the road so well, he dismisses it. In his mind, he is already at the factory hard top. We used to wake to the strain of metal and rubber, hearing them pushed toward another dimension. The air cracked with the roaring will of that truck to become a man's silent thought.

Women, not men, cut fish. Men unloaded the cold tanks, and bodies, wide-eyed with a surprise they no longer felt, ascended the conveyor belt that drummed down the length of the cutting room. Men heaved the cans into the trough above the belt. And men supervised the women's work.

Bullet was a supervisor. As we thrust our arms against the flow of fish and diverted a viscous school of herring onto our stainless steel sinks, as we cut the tails to resemble sardines, or sliced up to the gills for "fish steaks," our taped fingers holding scissors that had been honed to blades so sharp they could have shaved our legs; as we hurried to fill

93

our cans and to fill our trays with thirty filled cans, Bullet prowled the aisles, making sure we did everything just so.

He didn't hurry. Ash built up on his cigarette. Like a Fourth of July snake, the ash bent but did not break. Occasionally, he leaned toward one of us:

"Put another few in this can, Grace."

"Them's too big, Ida."

Women were paid by piecework. Some, the fastest among us, had a rhythm — lunging, snapping, gutting, placing — every gesture blurring with the next. Their feet scraped a two-step against the cement floor.

My cutting style was slow. How far from the caudal fin should I cut this fish so it will look like a sardine rather than a herring's tail? Here? Well, how about here? A bell rang and the belt stopped for the morning break, my second day on the job. The women loosened their plastic aprons and walked over to sit on the benches by the Coke machine. One, as she passed me, hissed:

"They'll fire you, sure thing."

"Why?"

"You're too slow, dearie. You ain't worth their money."

My fingers ached. The stomach acids of the fish had peeled away the skin on my palms. It was exhausting to stand up hour after hour. But I couldn't afford to lose the job.

There was a cutter, well into her eighties, who wore a red nylon wig that always slipped over one eye as she cut, revealing dark sprouts of hair at the back of her head. Her legs were as muscled as a runner's. She never looked tired. If she can do it, I thought, so can I.

At the break, a few women would gather around my sink, engaging me in quiet, formal talk. As if they barely noticed what their hands were doing, they would finish cutting the fish to complete my tray. At first, I was ashamed. Some were twice my age. I murmured how they should be resting, how I could finish up.

"We don't have much else to do, dearie. And besides, I don't like to sit," one answered. Moved by their kindness, I almost cried.

Like most of the women in the cutting room, I would have liked to become a "sniffer." Sniffers were better paid. They worked in the dark sorting room, smelling cans that were ready to be boxed and sent. Sniffers hunted, like bloodhounds, for that stray whiff of leaking, soured fish. Or, I thought, closing the blades of my scissors so gradually through a herring that the swollen entrails nudged against its scales, maybe I'd like to be president of the company. I'd change a few jobs, first thing. I'd see how Bullet cuts a fish.

The herring along our shore spawn in summer in shallow water. Because the fish were being netted so intensely year-round, the vast schools that used to number as many as three billion individuals were smaller in size and there were fewer of them. Factory boats from other countries plowed beyond the two hundred-mile limit. Our own boats, hounded by competition and a diminishing source, were picking up the fish on their spawning grounds.* They brought back in their holds herring that were swollen with eggs. When we cut into them, the eggs spurted out and clumped on our arms and aprons.

"I'm cutting up my daughter's job," commented one woman as she jabbed for another fish. By the end of the day, the eggs had dried into rubbery, itchy mats all over us.

No matter how the belt rattled and the cans clashed, the women talked.

"I seen him down there midnights, prowling about."

"And she shows her face 'round here."

"Yessah, don't care who knows it."

"Seems like her sister was just the same. And look how she turned out."

"He'll get his tail burned one of these days, fine and dandy."

"Did you know Mabel's been up to the hospital?"

"No. What ails her?"

"Pains."

When the last whistle blew, late afternoons, most of the women piled into the yellow factory van to be driven home. Gulls keeled around the factory. The waves sparkled. There was always a brisk, salty wind. I walked through the screaming birds, letting the wind blow away some of the smell of fish. On the Pond Road, I stopped to pick blueberries. I pulled off my sneakers and lowered my feet into the icy water of a stream. As I sat within the hot-baked smell of the evergreens, my sore feet in the wintry water, things came clean again.

*This practice is no longer allowed.

Chickens

One thing led to another in the mild September air of an afternoon three years ago. The smell of feathered bodies as they sank into the water of the scalding pot spread with startling intimacy over the garden. They hit the hot water with a hiss, were swished around, and then lifted out, feathers dripping, steaming.

Neighbors had decided to butcher six nonlayers. Each chicken had been carried firmly under the arm from its pen to the block, alert, silent, its neck extended. After the axe came down, the wings beat hard. The carcass, hoisted with a slipknot at the feet, flapped aimlessly in the air. Then, as if it had secured some final, satisfactory perch, it relaxed.

We plucked the feathers and drew out the organs. Gleaming ovaries spilled like heavy clusters of grapes, each grape larger than the one behind it. The first was flexible, its coating of shell translucent. The last was as small as a bead.

We had killed the wrong chickens. All over the garden feathers lay in clots. A party of surprised faces, a sprawl of feet, a harvest of eggs had come full stop by our boots. I discovered that it is too easy to disassemble something alive.

Perhaps it was the unsettled memory of that afternoon that made me, the next summer, order twenty-four chickens from the Feed and Seed Store in Ellsworth. Driving home with them in the car, windows shut to prevent drafts, my two children and I listened to their plaintive peeping. By the time we pulled into the driveway, our bonding was irreversible. We set them in a wooden box in an upstairs room. As we had read in a book on poultry management, we dipped each soft face to the water dish, then dipped it again into starter mash. They were thirty-six hours old. The book was rigorous about temperature: ninety-five degrees the first week, a tapering off by five degrees weekly. We lived, then, without electric power, which meant no lights to heat them, no electric covers.

We burned a cord of wood that April and the chicks thrived. At night we set a bean pot in the center of the box, piled their litter of pine shavings up against it, and filled it with hot water. Sometimes, as I had done when my children were infants, I woke in the dark. I stole into the stillness of that room to look at their shapes flopped down as if in Islamic prayer around the circumference of the pot, their wings, no bigger than my fingers, out to their sides.

At six weeks, soft contour feathers and crisp primaries covered them. We moved the chicks to a shed. Twelve were meat birds, their plumage so white, so pure, so sacrificial it cried out for blood. Early mornings, when the grass was still wet and the sun shining between the trunks of the trees, the white chickens were the first to push their way to the ramp. Slowly, with awkward dignity, they stepped down, one behind the other. Once on the grass, each radiant bird did a stolid dance — just a step or two, really, but enough for us to understand the ceremony in it, and perhaps, its intent. That small dance began our day.

The laying hens were black with copper breasts. They were thin and wiry. They leapt from the shed door, disdaining the careful ramp. Moving furtively in and out of the shadows like shadows themselves, they explored the details in the fallen logs and the debris of the deeper woods. Afternoons, they perched in the trees close by.

We let our chickens range. Under the firs they scratched up loose peat and took dust baths in it, flapping dirt over their feathers, their eyes glazed, ecstatic. They sprang after low-flying insects. They chased snakes. When a cat left a mouse on the doorstep, a chicken always found it. Snatching her prize, she ran, the others behind her, gaining, yanking at the grey fur. The victor swung around and disappeared beneath the house. There, headfirst in a corner, she rent the corpse and gorged on meat.

Having chickens had little to do with the prospect of eggs and fryers then. It had everything to do with seeing them unrestrained. Here, perhaps, in this patch of woods and brush, they were able to reconstruct from the distorted echoes of ancestry, rhythms of the jungle fowl.

Early September, migrating hawks glided over our clearing. Every day we saw sharp-shins or broad-wings. Anxiously we awaited the goshawks. We had read what Edward Howe Forbush, the noted ornithologist of the early twentieth century, had written about the gos.

Once this hawk had chased a chicken beneath the long skirts of a farmer's wife. She stood, horrified, as the hawk, a ruffled Rumpelstiltskin, pranced and dove about her hem. We read more Forbush and were not comforted: "Its attack is swift, furious and deadly. In the death grapple it clings to its victim, careless of its own safety until the unfortunate creature succumbs to its steely grip."

Inevitably, one morning our chickens scattered, shrieking. We bolted out the door and drove off a goshawk with a hail of stones. That afternoon it was back, angling in at a clip from the woodside. But it never caught a chicken. It must have grown sluggish on meals of young

grouse. Forbush would have been disappointed; it was teasing more than hunting.

We butchered our meat birds on a Sunday in October. The sky was an unworried blue. The day's ceremony began, as every other day that summer had, with the dance. It ended when I reached into body cavities, fingers over the warm masses slack beneath the bones. I drew them out like a sorcerer might, their full weight trembling onto newspaper. Before they dried and their color withered, I unwound them and read the secrets of my chickens' lives.

That night I dreamed of my own heart and lungs and liver, curious about the dark machinery in myself. It is a shame we cannot take a look, after we die, at who we were.

When the moon was bright on the snow that winter, the chicken shed looked like a gray stone standing by itself, throwing a black and perfect shadow on the crust; coyotes tiptoed to the edge of the trees and howled at it. The voice of a coyote at night wakes us instantly. Fear sizzles like a sparkler up the spine before the word "coyote" slides into the mind. We lay in bed with the moon flat on the sheets, imagining chickens pressed against each other in the cold, listening to those cries.

Our layers came with us when we moved to an old farmhouse in town. After they felt at home in their new shed, we let them into the yard. Ours were virgin hens. Too late, we noticed a gathering momentum at our neighbor's line. Twenty-four roosters, long-legged and randy, shuffled in the thin border of trees that separated the properties. Our soft hens padded across the grass.

We yelled. The outlaw herd broke loose. The roosters galloped over, grabbed the chaste hens by the backs of their necks, and mounted. We stood helpless as our innocent hens turned pliant before our eyes.

The neighbors butchered one of those roosters daily and hung it to a cedar branch above the chopping block. The carcass turned in the wind. Fewer roosters consorted with our hens. But one night, perched among them in the shed, we found a fugitive. His hackles, by flashlight, were long and thick, his back speckled, his wattles a deep fleshy red. He stood tight to the perch — a monarch seizing his throne.

We paid our neighbors four dollars for him and named him Henry. The hens would slip his iridescent feathers through their bills tenderly and peck with benign solicitude at his comb and the arch of his tail. He basked among them. A nervous, high-stepping stud, he could also be a gentleman, allowing his hens first pick through the morning grain or at the sweetest shoots of young grass. The hour before dawn, his muffled crowing tolled from inside the shed.

At a year of age he began to change — or perhaps to become more himself. He rushed the cats out for a brief, geriatric stroll. He chased the dog. He leapt at the children. The children protested his innocence, arguing that Henry was doing his job as he saw it. But as summer wore on, they bore long scratches and dark bruises on their legs. One afternoon, I cornered Henry near the water pan. I grabbed him. His curved spurs had grown too long; the points were tapered, hard. He was now what medieval breeders called a dunghill cock, not an aristocrat of the fighting pit, but a savage barnyard scrapper. As the children held him against the grass, I tried to cut off his spurs with a mat knife. They were as slick as horns on a bull. Finally, I severed one. The children cried out as blood spurted from the wound. Henry sighed deeply and closed his eyes.

Frantically, I wadded cotton over the rush of blood and wound tape around it. Pressure stopped the bleeding. We let go. He lay where he was as if our hands were still on him. Then he shot up and raced for the comfort of the hens.

Our chickens are two and a half years old now, so tame they lean over to instruct us before we pound a nail or pull a carrot. They give few eggs. Against the windbreak corners of the woodshed, they lie with Henry in the sun, gossiping in low, querulous voices.

When it is very cold, we hoe up their litter, loosen the clumps, make it light and friable again. We take them cracked corn and whole oats. We save them carrot tops. There is no sensible reason not to sharpen that axe and wheel that old maple block into the woods, under the cedars. After all, we killed chickens once. But a small reluctance holds us back. Hardly worth mentioning. Just the memory of the dance.

Sea Stars

On nights in late summer, wind barely ruffling the water, the tide pours over the sand as if it welled up from the basin of the bay itself. I hear it bubble as it separates and shifts the sand grains. When I kick along the edge of this cold flooding, diatoms phosphoresce like tiny matches struck, then instantly snuffed. Few places appear as peaceful as this, with the moon over the shoulder of a nearby cabin and yellow, soft lights of homes shining from across the bay.

I indulge myself: I allow myself to think that the hundreds of starfish that I saw basking in the low tide this afternoon might now pulse with that pure reflected brilliance of the stars in the sky, engaged in a serene dialogue, star matched to star. I let myself forget the pillage beneath this placid cover.

Near a bank of submerged rocks lie thick beds of blue mussels. The tide billows microscopic plankton over them. Their orange mantles frill beyond the rims of their shells. In the sparkling darkness, they draw in clean, cold water, and they feed.

I have come to remind myself. In the swelling water, I shine a light over the rocks. A starfish glides past my foot into the beam, mounts a mussel, braces its arms against the shells, and pulls. The mussel clamps. The relentless pressure from the starfish under the flashlight does not diminish. The mussel tires, loosens. Feeling the give, the starfish slips its diaphanous stomach from its body and nudges it between the shells. I can't see how the filmy stomach exudes a wash of digestive acid, dissolving the mussel's soft flesh, but I see the mussel weaken, gape wider. The stomach swishes inside the shells, bathing every part of its victim until all at once the mussel flaps wide, empty, except for a few scraps. Languidly, the starfish folds its stomach back into its body as if it were a dinner napkin, and moves on, oblivious to the night stars. A green crab tiptoes to one of the drifting shells and picks away at the last pieces as I climb the hill to bed.

Mute battles such as this one have been waged for over two hundred million years. Mesozoic starfish prowled the shallows of prehistory with other members of their phylum, most of which are extinct today. Starfish belong to a group of animals called echinoderms, or "spiny skins." All echinoderms live in the sea and most species frequent the tide line and the tidal pools. If you have walked the beaches of New England or waded the densely populated pools of Maine's granite coast, you have already met them. Sand dollars, scattered on low tide bars, are stamped with a delicate, five-petaled design. After a storm, leathery sea cucumbers wash up on shore in long knots of kelp. Green sea urchins graze on the algae in the pools, dozens of them blooming over the rocks like meadow thistles. If you are lucky, you may see the brittle star, a shy creature poking one of its skinny arms from its hiding place beneath a stone. The purple sun star, a deepwater echinoderm picked up by divers in the Gulf of Maine, is a ten-armed monster that can grow to be sixteen inches in diameter. Often the color of the star is so strong, the texture so encrusted, it seems a bejeweled covering, something to dry and cut and sew into robes worn by kings.

All these animals have bodies built around a five-point axis, or multiples thereof, and all of them move by ingestion and manipulation of seawater. "Starfish" is a misnomer, but one that will probably stick. Scientists prefer to call them "sea stars," for there is nothing fishlike about them.

Eight species of sea stars inhabit the waters of New England. Some, such as the sun star, are creatures of the polar seas, and as they range south, they take refuge in the depths off our coast. Stars that adapted to the Arctic seas are usually the ones that hold their young in brood pouches until they are old enough to prosper on their own. Stars of other waters release clouds of eggs and sperm. The larvae that result from this mass fertilization float freely as semitransparent wanderers, pushed by tidal currents until they acquire, through metamorphosis, their five-point shapes, and settle to the bottom.

The stars' rates of growth depend on food supply. If mussels, clams, and other bivalves are plentiful, the stars enlarge rapidly. But they can survive without eating for as long as two months. During lean times their size remains the same.

A hungry gull or a cod may pick up stars and eat them, but they

Sand dollar

are not a coveted item. As larvae, their numbers are naturally con-
trolled, for herring feast on the young, as do other schooling fishes.
Even the embattled mussel gets a taste of revenge as it siphons in newly
fertilized sea star eggs.

Although stars are not vertebrates and have no backbones, they
do have rigid plates beneath their skins, a coat of mail worn inside,
which gives them shape and strength. The sea star's nervous system is
merely a ring from which nerve cords radiate into the arms. There is no
brain. No one arm dominates. At each arm tip a minute nub protrudes
that is light-sensitive, the myopic equivalent of an eye. Many sensory
stalks lift from the sides of the arms like seeking fingers, reading by
touch information carried in the water. With only a nerve ring to

process what it has learned about the world immediately around it, it is puzzling how a star chooses direction. If the sensory stalks on all five arms felt the near and equal presence of oyster beds, it would seem that the starfish would freeze in a crisis of indecision. Yet it travels to mussels, clams, and oysters unerringly.

In an effort to save the shellfish beds, people once hacked the stars to pieces up and down this coast. After such carnage, star numbers mysteriously doubled, even tripled.

Echinoderms have an unsurpassed ability to regenerate parts. One dismembered sea star can become a constellation, so long as the severed arms bear a piece of the central disk. The men who tried to destroy them created enormous populations of healthy stars.

All sea stars have a sieve plate on their backs called the madreporite. Through it passes the seawater that flows into the tube feet of the underside. Set in four rows along the central groove of each arm, these cylindrical feet with sucker tips stretch and cling in synchrony, propelling the star over the terrain of the shallows. They create suction when they latch onto the shells of a mussel or clam exerting an even and continuous pull as they spell each other.

The bay I lived on is home to the most common shallow-water star north of Cape Cod: *Asterias vulgaris*. Under a microscope, the back of an *Asterias* looks like a landscape seen from an airplane — the approach, perhaps, into Santa Fe, going west into the sunset. The pink mesas and the bare, low hills are flushed with ebbing light. Peaks lift beside the narrow valleys smoothed by seasonal flooding — beautiful, and somehow, unearthly. But if one turns a more powerful lens to the eye of the scope, the Southwest vanishes. The back of the creature beneath the glass is dancing in rhythmic movement. Encircling calcareous spines that pop from the skin are tensile bulbs throbbing as they take in oxygen and release carbon dioxide. Scattered among them, pinchers open and close, bend and straighten. Their job is to remove anything that touches the star's back so that the respiratory bulbs can function.

Men who sought to protect the mollusk beds learned that these tiny pinchers will latch onto anything — even the strings of a mop. Mopping up sea stars sounds like a variation on the myth of Sisyphus, an unceasing, ineffective, exhausting task. But it is done, and it works.

I picked a star one afternoon at low tide and cut the nerve ring with a knife. After sawing through the tough skin, I set the star in a tide pool to watch the painless miracle: Three arms on one side of the broken ring and two on the other reached in opposite directions. The body lengthened, narrowed. Ever so slowly, it began to tear. One long afternoon, and the rip grew deeper, more ragged. Half-stars intent on their own rending slipped together over the lip of the pool at high tide. I watched the star go, knowing that soon each half would bud new arms and, before the end of summer, become a perfect five-point.

What will we dream on a still, radiant night like this one, above such stars as these?

Dragonflies and Nighthawks

They are gone. But I remember a slow, late-August evening, golden-edged — as if Aladdin had rubbed it to penumbral brightness — when a gathering of nighthawks and dragonflies took shape above our garden. They were feasting on winged ants. The nighthawks hunted near the tops of the trees. Dragonflies darted five feet above the garden. Gyrating in the warm air, a swarm of ants rose as black as cinders from an alchemist's fire.

More than a dozen dragonflies coursed over the garden. Their dry wings rasped through the gauzy stillness. Scissoring the light, they sliced angles above the last tomatoes heavy on the spent vines. They snapped into reverse over the carrot tops.

Ten birds flapped above the dragonflies on narrow, pointed wings, meeting the air softly. These wings suggest a falcon's, but nighthawks flutter like moths and swerve like bats trapped in a lighted room. The birds I was watching looked as if they had just been tossed from a sack, every which way, fighting for balance. Occasionally one called — a bleak, mechanical sound a wire might make when severed, suddenly, inside a large machine.

The nighthawks had probably nested on the flat rooftops of buildings in Ellsworth. I had heard them call at dusk all summer long. The dragonflies, abandoning their strict territories around neighborhood ponds, had become pilgrims like the birds, searching out the last insects before the hard frost. They were here as if by magic.

Nighthawks and dragonflies have always seemed magical to people — magical and sinister. Herdsmen once believed that these birds and their close relatives, the whip-poor-wills, sucked from the teats of lactating goats under the cover of darkness. A nighthawk's bill is a mere stub before a huge pink maw. It does seem as if it would fit well to a goat. Flying with its mouth open wide, the bird plows through hosts of winged ants, flies, mosquitoes, and moths the same way a baleen whale swims through krill.

American farmers used to blast nighthawks out of the air. Although they appeared gentle and harmless, they could not be, for they were called hawks and that was crime enough. Only when laws were passed to protect raptors did the shooting of nighthawks stop.

Folklore had it that the largest dragonflies, the darners, possessed extraordinary powers that led them to obstinate children who would not mend their ways. Before he could whisper "mumblety-peg," a naughty child might find that his ears had been stitched tight to his head by a darner. I remember as a child once stopping at the margin of a pond, checked by a dragonfly. What I felt, however briefly, was not fear but uneasiness. The tiny dragon moved by fits and starts. Its patrol was so swift, so erratic, that all I could see was a luminous blur.

We live in the shadows of the names we bestow. They are our curses and our charms. The magic of these animals does not lie in our make-believe, but in the fine-tuning of their adaptations to real dangers: cold and hunger and time.

Both the nighthawk and the dragonfly do their hunting on the wing and have evolved in parallel ways. The large, dark eyes of the nighthawk are set to the front of its head. Thus its vision has more binocular spread than a songbird's. It sees like an owl, able to judge distance and depth. The retinas of the nighthawk are replete with light-sensitive rods so that it can follow insects to the borders of the night.

The dragonfly, too, has a broad visual field. Anything flitting before it is tracked like an airplane across a radar screen. On my windowsill is the body of a darner that I found months ago, floating in the bay. It is as brittle as a pressed flower, its head almost all eye. These organs are considered marvels of the insect world, enormous for creatures so small. Looking at them under a hand lens, I can see they are made up of hexagonal shapes throughout (fifteen thousand to each eye, or so I have read). The hexagons are the tops of tubes that direct impressions to the optic nerves.

In neither animal are the legs adapted for walking. The legs of a dragonfly curve in upon one another and thrust forward. They bristle with short spines. The insect fashions a basket with its legs and scoops prey out of the air. The nighthawk's legs are hopelessly short, and its feet lack the articulation of a hawk's and, of course, bear no talons.

Perhaps the greatest irony for the nighthawk is that for so many years people shot them and never questioned how feet such as these could penetrate the feathers of a hen. As a matter of fact, a hen would make short work of a grounded nighthawk.

The wings of birds are modifications of forelimbs. Once they were legs and feet scuffing in the dirt. Whether a gradual change or a sudden genetic flash, it was an evolutionary afterthought to feather these limbs and make them beat at the air. Most paleontologists agree that Archaeopteryx, the first bird, must have used its feathered forearms to coast among stands of fern, plucking out insects and small reptiles hidden in the fronds.

Insect wings, however, did not evolve from legs. Fossils show that the first wing indicators were two flaps on an insect's upper thorax — a penchant for wings before the event. Etched in coal rests evidence of a Paleozoic dragonfly with a two-foot wingspan.

The dragonfly is the superior aerialist, outmaneuvering even the hummingbird, whose agility is legendary. Not only is it able to make instant changes of direction; it is also fast. Dragonflies have been clocked at forty miles per hour, which leaves the nighthawk in the dust.

The dragonfly may have speed, but nighthawks have endurance. Soon the birds I was watching would be gone, pulled south by an ancestral code that carries them over the Gulf to the shores of South America, crossing the mouth of the Amazon and on down until they reach the windy pampas of Argentina. They will lilt above the grasses long after the dragonflies here drop with the frost.

On that late-August evening, it took a glide of faith to believe that dragonflies perfected flight before birds knew little more than how to jump and to stretch.

Lorado's Marsh

The Toddy Pond Road in Surry follows the contour of the big, freshwater lake. Most people who travel it dismiss from their minds those brief, irregular glints of water on the opposite side, as if their minds had, momentarily, played them tricks. But behind a hedge of cattails lies Lorado Carter's marsh.

Mr. Carter was born in the farmhouse that sits on a rise in back of the flashing glimpses of water. From the house he looks out across a swath of mown fields to the heath, three long-dead trees holding osprey nests, and the water, rimmed with reeds and an army of cattails, moving sluggishly to the dam and through the culvert under his driveway.

For three burnished days this week of September, Robert and I have come to slosh around the circumference of the marsh to get a feel for it beyond what we can see with our binoculars.

There are many ways to look at a marsh. We will never see all of this one, never even see it quite the same if we look away and turn back again. At a distance, it is bands of color only: coppery sedges, then dry, pale cattail stalks, their brown seedheads unraveling. Above the cattails, the red maples are beginning to turn, and above them, the sky is a crisp, unequivocal blue. So is the water.

Almost a century ago, long before Lorado was born, this marsh was a mill pond. Logs were floated against the dam until they were ready for cutting. Soaking kept them free of beetle larvae. The barn where the big saws wailed is a skeleton today, collapsing quietly by the culvert. When the mill closed, the unkempt dam broke and the water poured away. The pond narrowed to a stream, dark and rich with the decay of the pond bottom. The water's pace quickened. It became a good place for trout. At the far end, the broad heath rose up.

As boys, on summer mornings, Lorado and his brothers used to sprawl upon a pyramid of granite, throw in their lines, and hook a mess of fish for breakfast. In time, trees grew to the edge of the stream. Alders curled above its banks. Then, in the spring of 1958, the beavers arrived.

They chose the dam site the sawyers had used. It was high-banked and bottle-necked, the right place to start holding back all that sweet-smelling, tannin-streaked water. They felled the saplings first, and then the alders. They girdled the larger trees and let them die. Tirelessly, they dragged branches with the leaves still waving on them to weave into the mix of mud and sticks and grasses and stones. The water deepened with the rise of the dam. The beavers ventured farther, felled more trees, and built wings up onto the banks to contain the seepage. Thick at the base and tapered to the crown, bowing downstream, the dam was a clean and solid job. Then they built themselves a lodge and settled in.

The water in the heath was rising. Half of the heath sank. The sphagnum, layered six feet deep or more, soaked up water like a gigantic sponge. Dislodged islands of sphagnum drifted, caught, and became places where seeds could sprout and grow. Underwater, black beds of peat spread.

Frogs colonized the wide, new shallows. They laid their eggs in the water as did the backswimmers, the predacious diving beetles, the water boatmen, the striders, and the whirligigs. They were only the front line. Within a few years, a rush of insects, animals, and plants had transformed the rising water and its wet receding banks into a place where every level, every corner of it was alive.

You can still see the old stream bed. It twists like a black ribbon sunk into the marsh's center, velvety with the shift of silt and the billowing growth of milfoil and algae. Stumps of the old trees punctuate the water. Branches stick up like the blunt heads of snapping turtles or the narrow bodies of basking otters. The rock where Lorado once caught breakfast sits mid-marsh, and on it — every morning these September days — a young great cormorant perches. We don't see many great cormorants, and very few this time of year. So we watch it preen the creamy feathers of its belly, snake its head over its back, and occasionally, almost sleepily, hold up both wings and wave them back and forth.

That rock, which has changed ownership more than once, will change again come nightfall. Raccoon spoor, grainy with the stones of

Painted turtle

fall berries, lies on the rock's summit. The raccoons must wade out over the pliant carpets of sphagnum and through the floating pondweed, digressing to feel with their fingers for the frogs and the insects hidden under the water. Perhaps they like to pass time on the rock and listen to the marsh sounds. Leaning back on their rumps like dancing bears, their front paws drawn up, they may raise their snouts and sniff at the cooling autumn air.

Who knows what we might see if we could sit here as long as the cormorant, or come at night like the raccoons. Our boots make sucking noises in the mud that alarm a flock of snipe. They zigzag out of our way, their rusty voices scraping the air. Two herons, alerted by the snipe, abandon their frog-stalking on the other shore. Their wings grazing the cattails on each downstroke, they depart reluctantly, like tired kings.

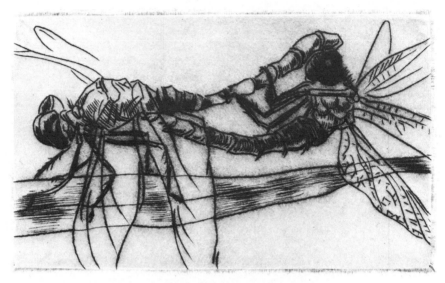

Dragonflies

We couldn't sneak up on anything here. The mud takes our boots to the rims. As we yank them out, young green frogs, assembled at the water's lacy fringe, yelp and plunge. The yelps and the splashes have a domino effect, advertising our presence in wavelets down the length of the shore. The frogs cry out the way small rubber toys do if you squeeze them quickly. One squeeze after another — and a hail of splashes.

We slosh up to places recently vacated. A neat bundle of cattail stems by a muskrat run tells us that this rodent has been out gathering. A mound like a child's mud pie, water still draining out of it, is a castor patty — the scent post of a beaver. Gray scats on the flattest rocks out in the brilliant wind-rippled water reveal the sunning spots of the eastern painted turtles. The turtles slide soundlessly into the water ahead of us and saucer away through the pondweed and the stalks of spatterdock.

We explore the beaver lodge. A rainless summer exposes it totally, no matter how frantic their damming. The entrances are no longer underwater, but yawn beneath the dome. From those dark holes, wide trails lead into the woods.

It must have been a hard summer for them. Lorado has seen otters cavorting in the marsh. These sleek and impetuous carnivores feed on beaver kits, as well as on muskrats, ducks, and fish.

The lodge at dry dock invites other predators, the raccoons and foxes, the stealthy fisher. Yet some beavers have survived despite the drought; their cuttings are everywhere. All summer long, Lorado has heard the sporadic crash of poplars.

We sit for a while on a smooth rock relinquished by the turtles. A lone osprey circles the marsh, lands for a moment in the bowl of a vacant nest, and then heads off to Toddy Pond. At my thumb an orange eft creeps from a crack in the granite. It is the terrestrial stage of the red-spotted newt. Hatched in the water, with feathery gills extending from the sides of its head, it matured to an eft and lived upon land for a year as this leather-skinned hunter of the leaf mold and weed thatch. Now it seeks water. Its skin will become silken again, a luminescent olive green with dark orange spots.

To look at the underwater bottom ooze takes an adjustment of the eye. If we wait, the blobs of scum and shifting sticks become pond snails, the cases of caddis fly larvae, the retracted body of a leech, a resting polliwog. The soft lap of the wind over the water barely interrupts their movements.

In summer, the spatterdock plant holds up its tight yellow blooms all over the marsh. Underwater, its stems are a forest tangle through which creatures crawl. The broad floating leaves create a canopy to hide beneath. Frogs squat on the leaves, and by fall, insects have chewed them to lace.

Now, all that is left of the spatterdock are seedpods, brown ragged leaves, and stems. I pull a stem up and its slime slides off between my fingers. That slime has a purpose. In a choppy fetch, the spatterdock stalks rub against each other. The transparent slime protects the dock from self-amputation.

Far away over the marsh the silhouettes of three hooded mergansers vanish in tandem behind a tangle of leatherleaf. A wood duck emerges from the other side. It hasn't seen us and so it approaches, its heraldic plumage in eclipse. By mistake, I move and the duck springs into the air.

But two dragonflies are not afraid of us. These common skimmers alight on Robert's hand hooked in a mating ring. The red male grasps the female at her prothorax, directly behind her head. The appendages of his abdomen tighten as if he planned to pop her head off like the cap on a bottle. Her abdomen hooks forward to his ventral side. In a slow, mesmerizing pulse, he passes her a tiny sperm packet, a white rectangle, an envelope, as we watch.

The View from Christy Hill

A low wave of fire moves across this ridge in the spring. It curls, breaks, and pulls away from the line of trees. For generations the land has been burned in the spring. Burning clears the weeds and sets the ash against the dirt to sweeten it. When blueberry land is burned, you can see it far off in the cold dark and for a second it ignites a sense of peril in the mind.

Midsummer, a spray plane drones over the flat slopes. A chemical mist hovers like smoke in the air and falls. But today the fields are clear. Only at a great distance where the land graduates into Blue Hill Bay, across Long Island and Bartlett Island to the smooth bulk of Cadillac Mountain, do low clouds impinge on the view.

In September, the pickers have gone. The strings that marked their raking lanes now unravel like the played-out threads of enfeebled spiders. Watery and sweet with fermentation, a few berries still hang on the plants. Bears are gone. Crickets scrape their tired songs.

Flying in from the poplars on the other side of the road, robins search for the berries and the crickets. Their orange breasts skim above the orange and pink and red leaves; they call to each other in a high, migratory nicker.

A month ago, these fields were host to huge congregations of robins. Above them, kestrels perched on the electric wire and in the old, dead spruce, their limpid eyes keen for an insect or a vole. As many as fifteen kestrels hunted over the fields by the hour. Cooper's hawks hunted the songbirds or cavorted in the constant sweep of the wind, rolling over each other, straightening out, coasting in slow grades, and disappearing between trees. Today a flicker probes the domed nests of the harvester ants. Its loud *wicka-wicka* carries in the still air.

The birds fly back and forth across the field to the spruce. Its jagged branches are perches for them to rest on and preen — vantage points from which they survey the fields. Although the spruce is dead — it has outlived four generations of Sedgwick farmers — it gives away only an occasional branch or strip of bark, black from the scorch of the spring fires. It plans to stand here forever, and so does the granite that lies scattered over the open ground, abandoned by a languishing glacier before there was anything like a Sedgwick farmer. Around the edges of some stones are signs of digging. The earth is loose, loamy. Rodents have constructed winter dens beneath the gray lintels.

In the sunlight, the dry leaves of blueberry plants lift like static flames. Cold nights destroyed the chlorophyll that gave them their standard green. Orange and red pigments prevail. Many of the leaves have already fallen to the ground. The thin, black stems and the drifting leaves crunch underfoot.

Wind moves stiff and shriveled bracken ferns, loosens the seeds of the flat-topped asters. Downy goldenrod raise their rusty, disintegrating tips.

The reach of the view from here is in miles. And for miles the emphasis of the woods has altered. Firs and spruces and pines, no longer obscured by lacy summer woods, dominate the lines and the contours of these fields.

Along the road a lone farmhouse faces the sun and looks out across the water, which glimmers in foreshortened perspective like a chain of silver puddles. It is a sensible place. Nothing frivolous. Nothing about it that could blow away in a wind or quit in an ice storm. It was built by men who were tempered by the fields they burned.

FALL

Coatue

A barrier beach is time's witness rising out of the sea, a spindly curb thrown up between habitable land and open water. There the days, the years, the millenia declare themselves. They bring offerings and lay them down, accumulations of ancient things, like glacial till, and passing things, like the seeds of plants. But a barrier beach is doomed to be swept away, the witness consumed by witnessing.

Coatue lies like an old bone against the island of Nantucket. Narrow and sharp, its sands shifting under the wind or with the water, it shields Nantucket Harbor from the northeast. The harbor water is gentled somewhat by its protection and, in turn, it protects plants and animals that could not survive the assault of the Sound. The waves that lap at Coatue's harbor flute its edges, carving a series of six points and half-circle coves. Across the sand, Nantucket Sound never calms. That water has no time for scenic coves. It lifts huge piles of sand and drives them up in a hump on the shore or takes them away so that they seem to vanish. But suddenly, underwater, they appear elsewhere as a shoal.

During the first week of September, when the sun was still as hot as it had been in August but the signs of a summer gone were everywhere, Robert and I rented a jeep and drove over the jeep trail to Coatue Point. Most people, I suppose, might choose a gentler place. We were drawn to that tense and fragile line where something, on the verge of becoming, verges on being destroyed.

It was 5:00 A.M. We were alone. The lines of jeeps that labor across the sands to Great Point, their deep-sea-fishing poles lashed to the roll bars, would not start up before daylight. The town of Wauwinet, where the trail begins, lay hushed under the moon's diminished light like a long-abandoned settlement.

The night began to seep away as Robert and I hit a zone of dead

123

sand and the jeep sank and pitched like an animal swimming. We followed the gleaming white tracks of the trail, lunging over black patches of low ground cover and around configurations of bushes. But for the water, we could have been on one of the great deserts of the Southwest. Water sounds were everywhere, filling the darkness like breath: a long inhale and a longer, rasped, slow exhalation.

The trail stopped on the back of a dune. We sat in a swale of beach grass, the Point melting down before us to the channel, and across the way, the ghostly shapes of the buildings of Nantucket town.

The wind, barreling over miles of open ocean, bullies this unguarded place. The beach grass around us thrashed. At our feet lay the restless debris of storms: driftwood and shell pieces, a string of whelk eggs, the leg and palmated foot of a diminutive sea bird — an alcid. We waited for sunrise as if waiting for an immense animal to open an eye.

An orange stain spread into the sky from behind a cloud bank hugging the water to the east. The wind shifted. Out of the Atlantic, the light glinted above the gray horizon and began to climb, spilling over Coskata Bluff. The light rolled toward us down the whole length of sand. As it pushed the darkness back, we saw Great Point, a brooding, eroded form hunched on the gray water like a flensed whale.

The light found our jeep. It awoke a Savannah sparrow, which flitted to the side-view mirror, chirped, and began to preen. I suppose there is little to surprise a sparrow here. Even a jeep can wash up from somewhere else.

As the sun swept across Coatue, colored it, made it shine in response, we remembered time: it took four thousand years to grind this sand and another six thousand years to sculpt it and seed it with the plants that hold it down.

Beach grass thrives on abuse. If the wind did not fling sand against the bases of its tough stems, it would die of too much gentleness. As it is, the wind never leaves it. Invigorated by the assault, it lowers a quick spread of roots. Other plants, spaced randomly over the Point, in the lee of the gradual slope away from the Sound, look as if they had crawled in under the cover of darkness. They keep a tight grip, as if they intended to outlast the wind.

The pods of the horn poppy ticked against each other. Dessicated and empty, their seeds that September morning had already dispersed. But a leftover yellow petal, as delicate and bright as a piece of party napkin, still clung to its stem. Around the poppies grew clusters of

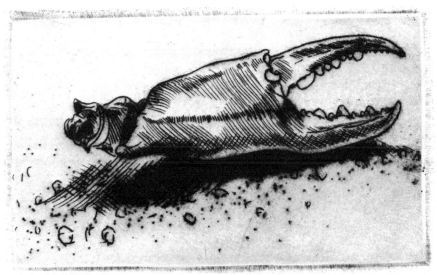

Blue crab claw

wormwood and dusty miller. When we walked through the grass, we found a cocklebur, crouched and secretive.

The island of Nantucket is a land of bog and moor. A Quaker island, it is Quaker-colored. The tints of deep purple, mustard, and russet of early fall are among the most beautiful in New England. On Coatue in September, colors are subtler still. And yet, like the horn poppy, a few plants show extravagant blooms in season as if, however briefly, they threw caution — literally — to the wind.

From the vantage of the berm, we saw the entire barrier beach, its sweep of beach grass and lichens, the flat, dark green poverty grass, the shiny black-green bearberry. An occasional seaside goldenrod stood out of the grass. Some purple thistles tossed their frothy heads. Little yellow asters, late flowers blooming just ahead of the autumn storms, scattered like trinkets forgotten by a child. Poison ivy lighted the sand in runs of deep, lacquered red. But the brown saltwort, the orache, and the pale sea rocket grew everywhere. And everywhere, like Quaker elders, they toned things down.

We kicked at a timber from a five-masted schooner that thrusts its bent and rusted spikes up through the sand. Beyond it, a jetty leans away from the beach, curving north. Another, which we saw on the other side of the harbor, runs parallel to the first, then away. These twin jetties, which are carefully maintained, hold Nantucket Harbor open to the sea. If they disappeared, sand would sift into the channel, choking the harbor neck in a season or two.

Across that channel sits the town, its white spires and gray shingled houses crisp against the brightening sky. It was toward these spires that two sailors trudged on the 6th of December, 1771, after their sloop cast up in a gale at Great Point. Two other sailors chose to walk out on the Wauwinet road, carrying between them the twelve-year-old cabin boy. Eventually, they found shelter in a barn. But the sailors who followed the length of Coatue were stopped by the channel. Within sight of the town, almost within earshot, but unable to arouse any notice, they curled up in the ice-coated sand and they died.

Coatue, Coskata, and Great Point, forming one continual sweep northeast, were once called "the chord of the bay" because they unwound together like a length of rope, or the backbone of an animal. But when one hears the wind through the grasses and the trees, one thinks of notes held, blending, harmonizing in a song. A siren's song. They hide a devil of underwater sandbars and tidal rips. Many ships have foundered here, their crews lost, their cargoes tumbling up the beaches days later. In 1883 a life-saving station was built at Coskata. The lighthouse at Great Point beamed its warning across the water through countless storms for 166 years. When a storm hit in 1984, islanders found, as the winds abated, that the lighthouse itself had crumbled.

Coatue is an Indian word meaning "at the pine woods." But the pine is gone. Every stick worth cutting was cut years ago. Thickets of twisted scrub oak rustle their stiff, coppery leaves. Red cedars lie under the full power of the wind. If it ever stopped blowing, these cedars wouldn't notice. They have tended southwest for so long, they are past seeking a direction of their own. At The Narrows, where sand separates Nantucket Sound from the harbor by less than a hundred and fifty yards, the cedars look as if they had tripped. Their trunks sprawl on the sand. The roots arch up, then plunge back down. The branches stretch from the trunks along the sand, grasping at the leaves.

Toward Five Fingered Point tall stems of a stand of panic grass bend together in a slow, undulant fetch. At the sound of the jeep, brilliant white heads of gulls popped up from the grass and looked us over. We stopped. This was not gull breeding territory, but a gull commons where the birds preened and rested. As we opened the jeep doors, the birds bolted out of the grass, extended their wings full-length, and let the wind pull them over the water. An effortless escape.

White pellets lay in the grass. They looked like primitive icons made by gatherers who worshipped the gods of flotsam and jetsam. They were gull ejecta, choked up by the birds after a full meal. We sat down in the grass like two gulls with time to spare, and pulled the pellets apart. Pieces of string came away from the tight wads, the vertebrae of fishes and splinters of shells crumbled in our fingers. We unfolded sheets of cellophane. Gulls will eat anything — but they are irresistibly drawn to the leavings of man.

Farther ahead, wooden signs warned us that we were on nesting territory. Under stunted copses of bayberry, oak, beach plum, and cedar, and tunneled close to the trunks, we found the gull nests. They are haphazard rings of beach grass. Empty shallow bowls, they mutely attested to the mating, incubation, raising of young, and recent dispersal. There are few things more desolate than a nesting area after the birds have gone. Immature herring gulls and black-backs had flown off with their parents. They would not return to these bushes until they were three or four years old. Then, their sense of a homing place comes back to them; they fight for territory under the branches where they were fledged.

Shells of the channeled and knobbed whelks, the common moon snail, and the shark's eye lay in the clutter. Their dense meat had been

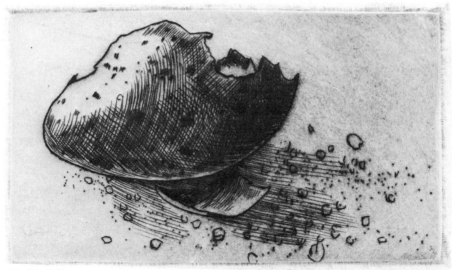

Gull's shell

Gull's skull

wrenched out and ripped apart to feed the ravenous chicks. Opercula, tough doors that close the mollusks into their shells when they are alive, littered the sand. Some are translucent. Others are callused. We held them up and they glowed as if sunlight came from inside them.

Bleached by salt and sun, the studded claws of hermit crabs, the carapaces of spider and green crabs, and the lady crabs — their polka dots only faintly visible — were strewn about the colony like ghosts, beautifully shaped, all color gone. The booty that the gulls brought ashore had been pillaged from the shallows. As fall approaches, most of these inshore creatures move into deeper water. Winter gulls scavenge dead and dying animals that wash up on the beaches. And, of course, they visit the island dump.

There were more than fifty nests here and another fifty or so farther down where a brushy trail leads to the bay. Reaching under a stand of oak, Robert carefully extracted a piece of eggshell. It was a mottled gray-green with brown spots: a camouflage egg.

This place was at once nursery and grave. Numbers of shredded bodies of gulls lay about the nests. Crippled by disease or injury, they had become food for the others. There are no carrion beetles here, no damp and moldering leaf bed into which the bodies of these birds can disintegrate. So, after they are gutted by their fellows, they lie here, their feathers ruffling in the wind. They become their own headstones.

In a season, drying under the sun, drying in the salt wind, at last mere husks, almost as weightless as a handful of jingle shells, they blow free.

In a rut of the trail we found the tail of a spiny dogfish, a small shark. The minute denticles in its skin are raspy growths. We thought at first it was a sandal strap. The skin curled over the place where the flesh once was. Sun-cured, it acquired an indestructible toughness.

On a knob of sand surrounded by seaside spurge, we parked the jeep again. A marsh hawk cut in front of us, its wings held at sharp angles above its body. We discovered its nest as we followed the base of a small rise where prickly pear cactus grows in patches. The nest was made of the stems of spartina grass, sticks, and the sharp culms of beach grass. Set close to the trail, it must have afforded the hawks a view of every vehicle that went by this summer. But the birds, blending with the ground cover, would have been hard to see. I pictured one of them, breast forward on the nest, which was as paltry as a discount Christmas wreath, its eyes, like wet, black stones, picking out a vehicle a long way down the sand, the head turning slightly as the jeep turned, the eyes following it, alert and ready, as if the jeep were a fox or a vole.

Near Coskata Pond, corridors of sand, once open to the tides but now sealed by dune wedges, retain depressions of still water. The shiny spartinas — the marsh grasses — meadow the wet sand. Glassworts and purple beach heather cluster around the brackish pools. Walking toward the pond, we stepped over retreating armies of fiddler crabs. At two inches in length, the male crabs are larger than the females. They each brandished an outsized, ceremonial claw, swinging it at us as if they could stave off our sneakers. Hundreds of pointed legs on tiptoe over the sand and hundreds of bubbling mouths sounded like a serpent withdrawing over the grass. Next to their burrows lay tidy piles of sand plugs. Architects of the banks they live in, these meticulous little animals carve the mud and the sand into an intricate, porous facade. Nutrients seep down to the spartina roots through the fiddlers' passageways.

At Head of the Harbor, we waded the shallow, weed-filled water. Eelgrass is a true seed plant and one of the few to grow in salt water. In the 1930s, it suffered a blight from South Carolina northward. Bays and harbors, once rich with it, became wastelands for many marine creatures. Although not yet back to its former abundance, the plant is recovering along the Atlantic coast. The gentle waters of Nantucket Harbor are lush with its green pastures. You would never imagine a blight here. The slow rhythms of its flat, wide stems keep the motion of the waves and follow the tidal shifts. To the eelgrass clung bay scallop larvae. Blowfish, their fins whirring like propellers, angled through it. Pipefish rested in its strands. Schools of shiners sprinted over it, just below the surface, just at the edge of the shore.

Coskata Pond, a trough through which the tides slide, is a cul-de-sac open only to the harbor. On its sandbars, the darkly mottled immature herring gulls mewed their hunger and lost dependencies. The adults were deaf to their cries. Young cunner, flounder, stickle-backs, and elvers that mature in the pond riffled the surface, igniting the interest of the gulls and the oyster catchers. Whimbrels, greater yellowlegs, and black-bellied plovers have stopped here on their long trek to the coast of South America to feed at the sandbars and down the points of Coatue.

The Coskata bluff, rising twelve to twenty feet above the east beach, is a crust of the old glacial moraine. On it, oaks and cedars meet the wind in one tight, cooperative contour as if they were a single tree. The bank is eroding. Some trees have fallen to the beach.

This place is kin to desert and tundra. Along its backbone, rain percolates through the top sand just as quickly as it would in a desert. The plants growing on these loose-grained rises and hollows are those that take up water fast, or store it, or maintain a root network that is deeper than most or broader. If you dug down at the dune base far enough, you would find that the water filling up your digging hole was probably saline. There are places on Coatue where fresh water can be had, but on most of it, salt limits what trees and bushes grow here just as permafrost limits growth on the tundra.

Tracks of domestic cats stippled the bare sand in a few places. Secretive and self-sufficient, these feral housecats, abandoned by their owners, take refuge in the sparse cover of this beach. It was hard to think of them as tabbys. They are the lean, wily hunters of the voles that dove for shelter under the fallen oak leaves as we passed by. They stalk the young of the western black-tailed jackrabbit, introduced to the island in 1925. These denizens of the Arizona deserts and the wastes of New Mexico are long-legged racers, at home on broad ex-panses of meager vegetation. Coatue suits them fine.

Great Point, like Coskata, is an exposure of the old moraine. The Atlantic thrashes it on one side, the Sound on the other. In the rays of the late afternoon sun an estuary glinted pinkly at its side. It held this year's

Oyster catcher

least and common terns. They stood in the brief water, bills piercing the solid flow of wind. The birds alternately lifted and were blown back, touched the water, lifted again, and flapped forward. They could not sit still. They brimmed with the energy of impending migration.

A monarch butterfly fought gamely down the beach. The wind punched it from side to side. It seemed to be the wind's toy, but it wasn't. Insubstantial, but with a will as strong as the wind's — or stronger — the monarch will journey to Mexico. This beach was only a small test.

We were almost off, sunburned, caked with a fine grit of sand, thirsty and bone-tired. We hardly watched the osprey coast over the jeep toward the manmade platform where its mate stood on the nest, facing into the wind and the sunset, the feathers of its head lifting.

Swirls of sea mist began to roll in off the ocean. They drifted across Coatue, erasing it. Abruptly it was gone. The island drew into itself. This was the beginning, thousands of years ago, before Coatue. Or it was the end, as the last sand was scooped up and carried off.

October on the River

We pushed off from the landing, turned the canoe north against the sleepy current, and set out on the Narraguagus toward the right fork. The canoe's aluminum prow cut the unruffled surface. At its stern, the incision drew together. A low wake spread. The water, sweeping off the paddle blades, splashed from the tips.

It seemed as if we had done this already, that it was merely an exercise in memory, as if one of us had pulled out of his pocket a wrinkled photograph, flattened it with a thumbnail against the kitchen table, and said, "Remember this?" There we were: Ada and Frank, the lunch between them, Robert, bent forward, paddling in the stern, I in the prow, my back to them. A pale sheen off the water lighted Ada's face beneath her straw hat.

The river curved gently. Tall grasses and rust-colored reeds grew on its banks. In back of the grasses, the noon light rose hazily out of the yellow leaves of the poplars and birch trees in the woods.

The early French Impressionists knew all about light like this, that it is apocryphal — it seems to come not from the sky, but from the things themselves. Suddenly, the surface of the water through which breaks the dying pickerelweed, the dry, waist-high grasses, the path that leads down to the common watering place, and the stumps of the trees are lighted by their own mortal fires.

It was too warm for October, too warm for the spare, nostalgic landscape. But the robins knew the season and could not be fooled. Migration brings out the best in them. Taut with a building excitement, they had been drawn in huge, erratic flocks to the river. Their shrieks and warbled whispers and the sharp *flup* of their wingstrokes met us at every bend. These robins — there were hundreds of them — were buff-colored, finely muted like everything around them.

133

In shallow fringes along the bank, the birds dipped down and splashed. Or they hung from the branches of the mountain ashes and the nannyberry bushes, plucking the frost-ruined fruit. Exclaiming, warning, darting across the river and back, they almost burst with the lust to be gone.

A river sets a true course. It never meanders. The loops and turns a river makes chart the path of least resistance, accounting for the slope of the land and the soil type it must displace to make its bed. The Narraguagus runs through glacial till and clay. There is not much slant to it, and so it rolls dreamlike toward Milbridge and the Narraguagus Bay.

Along the banks there are outwashes, places where the water sloshes into diversionary pockets, and pools there. Duckweed grows in this still water, as do pondweed and the water lily. A wood duck bolted out of one of them. Its white facial lines, white belly, and lovely head-high thrust were unmistakable. As it flew, it uttered a peculiar little cry.

After an hour or so, we became tired of wood ducks. They blasted out of every shallow pond and whirred to pools up ahead. Listening to our paddles and lazy talk, they would stop dabbling, freeze on the water, and, as we approached, rocket away once more.

Cuttings of beaver drifted against the banks. We saw no new lodge, but the banks, exposed by a summer of little rain, were tunneled. Into those large holes, branches had been tugged. The animals worked the banks vigorously. The mud looked scratched and ledged.

Four gunshots ripped the silence. A black duck bellied over the tall grass, found the river's path, and followed it. The duck quacked as it flew. Its alarm faded away to silence.

We let the canoe drift to the shore where a trapper's cabin perched on a hillock. We disembarked and walked a lumpy furrow through the grasses. It brought us up to a window. Although the outside walls of the cabin seemed adequate to deflect the rain, the inside had been ravaged. Most of the floor lay in splinters, exposing dirt between rotted sills. The hearth and chimney disintegrated against one wall. The walls themselves were gouged and shredded as if a beast had been locked in against its will.

A bed made out of planks was hammered into the far wall, half-way between what used to be the floor and the ceiling. If one were to sleep there, the way to do it would be to leap from the front door across twelve feet of cabin. Curiously, a cement hole opened beneath the bed.

Wood duck

No matter how tired, one might hesitate before leaping. Anything might come up from that hole at night. Or go down.

There is little dissembling in this river. By early afternoon, we knew the temperament of the north fork of the Narraguagus. A typical down-easter, the taciturn flow of water goes about its business with barely a ripple.

We came to a gravel bar extending in a half-moon around a slow bend. It was two o'clock by our watches, although by the vaporous air, it could have been an early morning in August on the Loire, or a September evening on the Suwannee stretching out as interminably as a Georgia lady's drawl. We dragged the canoe onto the bar.

Tracks covered the gravel: the clefts of deer, the handprints of raccoons, the webbed press of beaver paws. Large, undefined marks suggested that a bear had ambled down to the water. Crows had paced back and forth here, checking over everything.

Ada served lunch. One of those special few who think of lunch as a minor art form, she knows how to celebrate the small rituals of hunger and appeasement. The wine, the color of this October light, was cold and sharp against our teeth, a presage of winter.

Lying back on the gravel, I listened to the black ducks quacking around the bend. The opposite bank rose steeply from a slight lip of earth extending into the tannin-streaked water. Erosion had hollowed the bank. It was as ragged as a gnawed apple core. A stiff mat of roots hung over its top. Behind the roots lifted a grove of trees. One tree, a birch, hung down over the bank and was growing perpendicular to it, held by a life line of roots and aiming its crown at us like a cannon. The tree had summoned energy to leaf. A few brave yellow flags spun on its branches.

Three tamaracks at the river's edge curled in unison away from the water, away from the light of the sun. It was an unnatural bending. Exempt from the everyday rules that govern everyday trees, they made the incurved arc together, their tips gesturing toward the trees above them. As I closed my eyes I wondered if perhaps they were signaling to us that they wanted to be with the others up in the grove. Perhaps, I thought, we should paddle over and drag them to the top. Perhaps they were even shrieking at us to do so — for how faintly the shriek of a tree might fall upon a human ear.

The sun's heat was warming the air above the gravel bar. Frank and Robert and Ada discussed the three trees, suggesting that they must have hung by their roots like the birch for years, time enough for their trunks to bow, reaching for the sky. Then they skidded down the bank together. As they fell, their severed roots seized the land by the water and held. If that is their history, those trees have had three lives: one as saplings in the grove, a second, clinging to the eroded bank, and now, the third, here at the water's edge. Charmed trees.

The question of the trees settled, the talk drifted to something else. I was falling asleep. I opened my eyes and saw a gaping hole beneath a poplar to one side of the opposite bank. Big enough for a bear. And then, closing my eyes, I thought of a bear's sleep, wondering whether bears in hibernation store with their fat days like this one, so they can play them back in dreams.

November

Skim ice set around the pond's edge last night. There has been ice here mornings, but this looks as if it will stay. Not enough warmth predicted come noon to melt it. It rays out in sharp points toward the deep center, looking more like decoration than what it really is. In truth, it is a runner, come from the far north field with a message: Your troops have been routed, have fled. Prepare. Our forces muster on the near hill.

The ice is transparent, still. The wind cannot stir it up. Beneath it, as if they were in a bowl, three goldfish hang in the dark water. Pieces of cedar spray mar the smoothness here and there. Narrow shafts of sun reach through the white pines and play upon it. When I break a shard of ice off, it melts between my fingers almost at once, flashing with the sun's early light as if it had been set afire.

These fish understand the seriousness of ice. The temperature around them has dropped. To rise toward ice would mean traveling into colder layers, right up to the freezing point. Their machines have slowed. They won't pick up again until the ice is off. The blood that flows through a fish is thick; it holds less oxygen than ours. A cold red sludge thumping slowly through the animal all winter, it will keep the fish barely alive.

Fish aren't the only ones who know ice. That huge granite rock, halfway down the yard's slope, a mountain spur left by the last glacier — it knows. Its posture — a look of action arrested — implies that it is mid-journey, pausing before the next grand thrust.

The white birches swinging their bare heads over the west field know about ice. I have heard them crack when the water in their cells froze in a hard, nighttime January wind. The sapwood contracted suddenly, tearing the wood in a thin slash to the heart.

We carry so much water within: the fish, the trees, ourselves.

I have a book that explains that water came, originally, from stone. As the earth cooled and crusted over, vapor turned to water and was caught in rock. Then the rocks sprang leaks and the first water gushed free. I have another book that mentions that although we find water tasteless and odorless, a creature from another planet that did not have water in its own body might find it vile-tasting, evil-smelling stuff.

We know it for the purest thing on all the earth when it is clean, the most comforting thing on earth when it is warm and still, and the most dangerous when it turns cold. Even before it transforms to ice or snow, cold water can suck the heat out of a human core the way a kid sips a shake through a straw.

What would a creature from another planet make of ice around this pond? Would it be taken for a warning? Probably not. Probably only we who carry small seas within can fear this cold.

December

The tide is out. Down the long length of the bay where darkness gathers as if it were building up behind a dam, the wind brings in a scattered mix of rain and sleet. The rocks and the mud flat and the air seem deserted by all living things — almost all, for I have chosen to walk this way before dark and a lone crow has chosen to poke among the rock debris over where the channel unwinds through the gray and faintly luminous mud.

Aren't the crow and I too smart to get caught in such a place when everyone else has left? That bird can master simple numerical puzzles and likes rhythm as much as any drummer. It is able to remember and to play tricks. Why didn't that crow go south?

Bands of crows crossed over this bay in September, migrating south from inland nesting sites. They joined up with the birds that had summered here. One pair had nested in the ragged copse of mixed evergreens where a creek, no wider than a crow's wingspan, flows sleepily into the marsh.

We found out that the crows were nesting close to the house by accident. Crow call is a common summer noise. Usually, the *Craaack-caa-ca-ca-haaa-ha-ha* ragtime announces as far as the voice can carry the energetic audacity of the bird. But for two days, crow-scream issued from one spot in the woods. The cries were higher than normal, and constant. Suddenly we knew they meant "Terrible!" "Injury!"

We don't speak crow. But we recognized those sounds. Elemental emotions such as pain and fear and pleasure are the Esperanto of the animal world.

After searching beneath the lamentations and the frantic diving flights of the birds, we found the beheaded and gutted body of a nestling. Except for the feathers still held in their blue-gray sheaths, the body looked like a small chicken, cleaned and ready for the oven. We found another kill, and close to it one brown-checked contour feather. It was as clear and incriminating as a paw-print: the flying tiger. The great horned owl.

One by one, the big bird must have picked off the young by night until the crows abandoned their nest, then their outrage, and at last the woods became silent.

Hundreds of miles from here, as the dusk comes on, crows are winging to their ancient winter roosts. On Pea Patch Island in the Delaware River, over 500,000 crows used to sleep tight to the branches of the trees. If that roost has not been destroyed by men — or by owls — perhaps the crows that left this bay are funneling down to Pea Patch now, as I walk toward this stubborn die-hard. This crow that would not go.

The bird flops a stone over and gouges its beak into the mud. It grabs a clam worm, swishes it clean in a puddle, and chokes it down. Because the day is almost gone and I have walked too close, the crow flies. It crosses the expanse of mud, heading toward the trees on the other side of the bay. *Wa-ha-ha-cowakle-cowakle* it calls back. Another crow salutes from farther down the bay.

I turn to the road and the sleet hits like sand in the wind. Why do we stay?

Tomorrow, I should ask that crow.

A Pair of Osprey

"You folks planning to post this land?"

It was the week before the first day of hunting season. The man stood splay-footed, holding his gun slack in his hand with the muzzle pointed to the ground.

"We don't want hunting," said Robert evenly.

"No sign'll keep me off it. Any posting and I'll be setting tight to your roof with my flashlight waiting for a deer to come to them apple trees." He nodded with the side of his head to the two wild castoffs, small, rangy trees at the garden's edge.

"I been hunting this land back to the Winter Harbor line for years. My father hunted it. There's men from this town not willing to turn back at somebody's sign all of a sudden."

"You'll be breaking the law."

"You folks from away moving in like you own the place. Well," he smiled — a tight, sharp gesture — "You don't."

We knew the land was ours, of course. The papers that said it were folded in an envelope in a safe deposit box in a town thirty miles away. But we couldn't stop him. We couldn't stop deer driving either, when a fan of men hooting in the dark like crazed owls pushed a herd toward the road where other men waited, crouched in the bush with their guns cocked.

A truck when it grinds over the meadow doesn't sound like one headed up the road. Even at our distance, we could hear the effort it made, in low gear, slapping over the ant hills and across bare granite. We heard the motor switch off. The truck waited for dark like a poised beast, the light on its hood ready to aim its enormous, paralyzing eye, the high-powered guns bristling from the windows of the cab. At night the does came with their fawns to eat the few scabby apples.

In fall, when hard frosts had iced the ground under the trees, we could sometimes hear coon dogs at night. The packs advanced from the road, over the fields and into the woods, singing after raccoon.

One night a coon dog yawled until dawn from one corner of the woods. It was trapped. We found its owner lugging it out as the sun rose, bloody, its tongue dragging between its foaming jaws and its eyes rolling like a frightened calf's.

"Wild animals don't feel pain. They're just not like you or me."

They aren't like that hunter's dog, either. When trapped, they don't make a sound. Robert and I didn't know much about the wild animals that lived on the land we bought. We were learning.

That same first year, a neighbor tramped the crusted path between his house and Forbes Pond, carrying out every last beaver we had watched all summer long. Over his shoulder, their frozen bodies stuck out like cordwood. His kitchen had a close, sweet smell. The scent glands of beaver hung from a clothesline above his cookstove — dark, twisted bulbs of flesh that he would smear over the steel traps before he set them.

"Creatures are put here for us to use. Why else do you suppose God made 'em?" he told us. But he thought, at our age, we should have known.

Outside his house the peeled bodies of beaver lay on the snow by the doghouse. Dog food. Nothing looks quite as naked as an animal without its pelt. The pink, plump flesh wrapped in a net of blue veins might be a naked plastic doll but for the veins and the white sheen on the pink that made the flesh look wet and real. The unlidded eyes popped in embarrassed disbelief.

Wherever we looked, in those years, man had tampered. We found cumbersome, dappled bodies of harbor seals that had drifted into the coves near our house, bullet holes in their heads. We found songbirds wounded by BBs. A loon was brought to the sanctuary, its lower bill blasted off. Robert killed a barred owl with both wings and both legs broken from gunshot.

If you live in a place, believing something that no one else believes, you pickle; you turn sour. We were never completely alone, but there were so few of us. I remember one woman rescuing waterlogged eiders coated with soy oil from the sardine cannery. She carried them, like children out of an earthquake, into her immaculate living room, and bedded them down in cardboard boxes by her parlor stove. The wildlife ranger who came to collect them didn't have the heart to tell her they would all die. I remember a warden tracking canoeists for hours along the bay and serving them a warrant as they docked.

"They raked that scoter as it sat on the water — wouldn't let it rise. It just gave up finally and lay stretched out on a wave. Then they killed it. And all the while with their son looking on. I imagine he must be some proud."

But I think things are beginning to change. I believe we are at last willing to recognize limits and value.

A pair of ospreys has fished the bay we live by, nested and raised young here. When reclaiming territory each spring, these raptors drift out, skimming the treetops. Every fall, with their newly fledged young, they belly on the warm air that balloons over the water.

Ospreys can live for twenty years. They mate for life. For a long time it looked as if they would not be able to breed again successfully on the East coast. But they have survived DDT and the clearing and settling of their traditional nesting areas. In Maine, ospreys repopulate their former sites. And people care.

In September, a repairman from the telephone company stopped to tell us that one of the ospreys had been electrocuted by our power line. He showed us the feathers tufted to the transformer that had killed it. At our feet by the pole, the big bird stirred as if sleeping. Maggots pulsed in its belly, eating it clean.

Neighbors heard about it and stopped to see the body we left by the pole. They had lost the pleasure of seeing this bird in the air above their homes, year after year.

Find Your Luck Slowly

Forget roadside crossings,
Go nowhere with guns.
Go elsewhere your own way,

Lonely and wanting. Or
stay and be early:
next to deep woods

inhabit old orchards.
All clearings promise.
Sunrise is good,

and fog before sun.
Expect nothing always;
find your luck slowly . . .

Philip Booth
"How to See Deer"

This country has a history of people who entered into wilderness not to beat it into submission, but to be changed and challenged by what they saw. The writings of many, including John Muir, Aldo Leopold, George Miksch Sutton, Edwin Way Teale, Loren Eiseley, Rachel Carson, and of course, Henry David Thoreau, attest to this. They have described what nature chose to reveal to them; they have taught us to go and see it for ourselves.

Loren Eiseley wrote: ". . . man is an intruder into silence. The light must be right, and the observer must remain unseen. No man sets up such an experiment. What he sees, he sees by chance."

Our terrier completed our walk along the borders of the deserted hayfields yesterday — a walk from which she takes her digressions and long-cuts — with the front leg of a porcupine held primly between her teeth. A reluctant hunter, the dog obviously had found this treasure already severed from the whole. The leg must have belonged to the porcupine that lived all winter in a hollow under the marsh bank. Through the snow months, the animal steadily denuded the trunk and branches of the white pine whose roots formed the struts in the walls of its dwelling. Despite the damage it had caused the tree, I liked the porcupine. I had a proprietary interest in its slow insatiability. It was the first animal we ever saw on this land, other than the two red squirrels that live by the road. We thought of the porcupine as "ours."

I wanted to know how it had died — or, more precisely, I insisted upon knowing, as if I had a legal right to that information by virtue of my deed. It could have been skewered by a great horned owl, in which case I might find signs of struggle. If a fisher tricked it into revealing its soft, unguarded belly, there would be fur left, and bones. Even if a bear, hungry for its first spring meat, dared to cuff it, there would be evidence.

To help me read the last page of this porcupine's story, I led the terrier back to the bank. I wanted it completed, neat. The dog snuffled over some moss, turned down into a gully, and ambled away after a stale scent. I backtracked in the woods. I looked under the branches of the firs that rested on the ground, and kicked through last year's marsh grass. There was no sign.

Of course, Eiseley is right: one cannot force chance. If the body lies somewhere, its secret belongs to carrion beetles, to the peregrinations of the skunk (the air is spiced with a faint skunk smell), the woodland mice, and the pigmy shrews — but not to me.

It is a stubborn lesson, this learning to relinquish the questions of the moment because the answers will not be given on command. One must tame the distractions of one's mind. I remember Edwin Way Teale writing of his abandoned orchard and how he would sit in the tall grasses day after day, learning from the insects continuing the purposes of their lives around and over him. He asked nothing of them. He sat and he watched.

Emerson warns that nature is not a toy. It has its own irrepressible rhythms. It has mystery. It gives to those who take initiative and practice patience. And what do we gain from all this? Perhaps it is something like Thoreau felt, after wandering the borders of his pond, watching the seasons play out before him. He could say at last, "I go and come with a strange liberty."

One steely December afternoon, I finished Annie Dillard's *Pilgrim at Tinker Creek* and was driven by her words out of the house, up through the maple stand, and into the tangle of evergreens that grows along the old town line. I wanted to *see* something. As dusk filtered deeply into the already dark trees, there was a stir in the snow ahead. A barred owl rose off the crust.

The frozen body of a hare lay partially uncovered, and around it was a faint press of wings like the "snow angels" my children used to make. I retreated into the woods and sat down on an ice-covered stump to wait. The owl would come back and tear at the thin, ravaged carcass. It was only a matter of time. I was willing to sit forever. A layer of ice beneath me turned to water, seeped into my jeans, and froze again, fastening me to the stump. A leg fell asleep.

After awhile, I turned cautiously around. The owl was perched in a tree at my back. It had been there, I suppose, as long as I had — watching me. The big bird gave a jump, fanned out its wings, and disappeared. I pried myself off the stump and trudged home.

Occasionally, there are gifts. Annie Dillard watched a frog doing a perfect dead-man's-float on the surface of a pond as a giant water bug hung onto the frog's belly and sucked it empty from underneath. She sat still as a muskrat gathered grass at her feet.

I have seen a male purple finch rip up a tuft of weeds and hold it in his bill and spin along the ground toward his mate, singing ecstatically all the while. I have seen an ovenbird lead its young over a log, single file. Once, I saw two otters at play. So we go out again, collecting moments from others' lives, allowing our lives to touch against something wild.

A year from now I may find the bones of the porcupine scoured by the seasons and the appetites of other animals. Then I will pick them up and try to guess again what happened. Life at the bank and in the marsh, under the flat light of the full moon and over and under the disintegrating trunks of these fallen trees is mine not by right or deed, but only if I see it. A question — as Philip Booth would have it — of finding one's luck slowly.